Regional Tourism

Regional Tourism

B.S. Badan
Harish Bhatt

Commonwealth

[The responsibility for the facts stated, conclusions reached and plagiarism, if any, in this book is entirely that of the Author. And the Publisher bears no responsibility for them, whatsoever.]

Regional Tourism

First Published : 2007

ISBN 81-311-0075-8

Published by :

Ajay Verma
For COMMONWEALTH PUBLISHERS
4831/24, Prahlad Street,
Ansari Road, Darya Ganj,
New Delhi - 110002
Ph. : 23272541, 23257835
Fax : 91- 011- 23257835
e-mail : campusbooks@hotmail.com

Printed at :
Roshan Offset Printers
Delhi

PREFACE

Tourism can be defined as the act of travel for the purpose of recreation, and the provision of services for this act. It is a service industry, comprising a number of tangible and intangible components. The tangible elements include transportation systems—air, rail, road, water and now, space; hospitality services, accommodation, foods and beverages, tours, souvenirs; and related services such as banking, insurance and safety and security. The intangible elements include: rest and relaxation, culture, escape, adventure, new and different experiences.

Travel and tourism is a major industry in the world and is at the top of the league of invisible earners of foreign currency. Many sovereignties, along with their respective countries and states, depend heavily upon travel expenditures by foreigners as a source of taxation and income for the enterprises that sell services to these travellers. Consequently the development of tourism is often a strategy employed either by a non-governmental organization or a governmental agency to promote a particular region for the purpose of increasing commerce through exporting goods and services to non-locals.

During recent years the tourism industry has witnessed unprecedented growth. Increasing consumer demand for educational and participatory travel experiences has resulted in a variety of specialty niche markets such as ecotourism, cultural-heritage tourism, and agritourism. New paradigms link strategic tourism planning with sustainable development.

The leisure and tourism industry is one of the leading global economic activities, a multi-billion-dollar industry with

700 million international travellers per year around the world. Tourism is a motor for employment and income creation and, especially in poor countries, a vehicle for development. But today it is not sufficient to simply create employment without regard for the quality of jobs and the social and environmental effects of tourism in vulnerable areas. A growing number of organizations, including the tourism industry leadership, are increasingly conscious of the risks and are adopting a more responsible attitude.

The present publication provides an authoritative look at how to manage travel and tourism industry in a better way. It introduces the complexities of the tourism system so that they will be better positioned to eventually assume the managerial challenges and responsibilities in a diverse and challenging industry. The latest advancements in tourism theory and thinking, retaining the thoroughness of content, diversity of applications, regional and international issues, economic significance, tourism operators and the role of technology in the tourism industry etc. are also described elaborately. Numerous regional and global case studies and examples are included to provide an appropriately broad geographic context. This work will be highly informative and useful to students, researchers, policy makers, managers and working groups of travel and tourism industry.

B.S. Badan
Harish Bhatt

Contents

1

A History of Tourism

Introduction

It is generally accepted that the roots of modern, mass tourism lie in the social and economic changes that occurred during the nineteenth and twentieth centuries. Certainly, technological innovation provided the means for faster, safer, more reliable and cheaper travel, whilst increasing levels of personal income and greater amounts of free time meant that more people could participate in tourism. At the same time, changes in the way people lived and worked, resulting in particular from rapid industrialisation and urbanisation during the 1800s, created the need or desire to go on holiday. Thus, it is not surprising that tourism is often considered a phenomenon of modern times.

Tourism is also generally regarded as a European and, more specifically, a British 'invention'. That is, it is often claimed that Britain played a dominant role in the evolution of tourism with, for example, the emergence of resort-based tourism (in spa towns and at the seaside) setting the patterns of tourism, whilst technological advances combined with the entrepreneurial talents of travel 'organisers', in particular Thomas Cook enabled increasing numbers of people to become tourists.

However, both of these perceptions are largely incorrect. Although it is only relatively recently that tourism, especially international tourism, has become an activity that the majority of people (at least in the wealthier developed countries) can enjoy, people have been able to travel for as long as there have been the means to do so. The first sea-going ships were designed and built some 5000 years ago and people have been 'tourists', travelling for education, pleasure or spiritual fulfilment, for as long as they have been physically able to travel from one place to another. Nor, of course, was Britain the only country that was instrumental in the evolution of tourism. Many other countries and societies, in both modern and ancient times, have contributed to the emergence of tourism, although it is probably the history of tourism in Europe that is best documented in the literature (see, for example, Towner 1996).

Nevertheless, a British perspective on the evolution of tourism provides a basis for understanding how and why tourism has, in general, become the global phenomenon that it is today. More specifically, it also demonstrates how tourism has become increasingly 'democratised'—that is, available, to and enjoyed by the masses—in a pattern that is being repeated to this day in other parts of the world. Therefore, this chapter focuses on the contribution of Britain to the evolution of tourism, highlighting specific periods and influences that provided the foundation for modern-day tourism. First, however, it introduces the subject by looking briefly at early forms of tourism.

Tourism in Ancient Times

From the earliest times, two factors inhibited the growth of tourism, namely, the difficulty or danger of travelling and, for the majority, a lack of money. Typically, travel by ship was the safest and most convenient mode of transport and was primarily motivated by either trade or warfare—opportunities to travel for pleasure were extremely rare. Nevertheless, the ancient Greeks enjoyed tourism of a sort, through primarily for religious or sporting purposes or for consulting oracles. For example, the oracle at Delphi drew people from far and wide to seek advice on various matters whilst the Pythian Games, also at Delphi, were a popular event. However, it was Olympia, home of the Olympic Games, that was probably one of the most popular destinations of the time. The first Games were held in 776 BC and, thereafter, attracted thousands of visitors from home and abroad to witness the sports and other events which gave the Games their deep religious significance. Indeed, tourism to the ancient Greeks was not leisure, but 'a trip in accordance with tradition and ritual. The man who travelled tightened his links rather than liberated himself from his social background' (Sigaux 1966: 10).

Tourism and the Romans

It was the Romans who first overcame one of the major hurdles to the development of tourism by developing a road network across the Empire. This not only allowed for the rapid movement of troops and administrative personnel but also increased the opportunity for private individuals to travel. By the first century AD, it was possible to travel along paved roads all the way from Hadrian's Wall in the north to the southern edge of the Empire in Africa, with travellers being able to break their journey at staging posts, or hotels, along the route. However, travel remained primarily for the purpose of trade or military service, with only wealthier Romans able to travel internationally for pleasure.

In contrast to the philosophy of the Ancient Greeks, tourism for the Romans became a form of leisure and escape. For those who could afford it, 'second home ownership became a way of avoiding the summer heat of Rome, whilst the building of the road network led to the development of a number of resorts along the Bay of Naples. Through a process that was to be repeated around the Mediterranean some 2000 years later, small fishing villages were transformed into bustling seaside resorts where excessive drinking, loud parties and nude bathing were commonplace. Thus, whereas previously tourism had been for the purpose of trade, health or religion, the Romans introduced the concept of tourism as a means of escape pleasure and self-indulgence, a form of tourism that disappeared with the decline of the Roman Empire during the fifth century AD and which would not reappear until the twentieth century. In fact, the tourism as a leisure activity was to disappear for almost a thousand years, although other forms of travel and tourism were to emerge in the intervening period.

Tourism in the Middle Ages

Following the collapse of the Roman Empire, travel became more difficult and hazardous and, generally, few people had the means, opportunity or desire to travel. As a result, tourism, such as it existed at this time, was limited to local fairs, festivals and religious holidays (or 'holy days', from which the word holiday is derived), with longer journeys usually being for the purpose of trade.

Nevertheless, one popular form of 'voluntary' travel during this period was pilgrimage. 'In its purest form, pilgrimage was a voluntary journey to worship at some holy shrine, and the journey itself was expected to be hard and fraught with difficulties, as a form of penance' (Jubb 1986: 3). Although such journeys had been undertaken since the third century, during the Middle Ages increasing numbers of people set out on pilgrimages, mostly on foot, usually to one of the three most popular destinations of Jerusalem, Rome and Santiago de Compostella in north west Spain. By 1300, for example, an estimated 300,000 pilgrims visited Rome each year although shorter, domestic trips were also popular, such as English pilgrimages to Canterbury or Winchester. Interestingly, the trip to Santiago de Compostella is once again a popular walking route, though principally as a long distance walk rather than a journey of spiritual significance.

Tourism between 1600 and 1800

Whereas the earlier periods are of interest in their own right, the seventeenth and eighteenth centuries are of more importance in the historical development of modern tourism. Although they preceded the modernisation and industrialisation of society, it was during this period that the pattern of tourism development through to the present time was established. In particular, it was then that the democratisation of tourism began, a process that has culminated with the mass participation in tourism that we know today.

Fuelling this process were a variety of factors that were, and remain, essential for tourism to flourish. In other words, tourism, 'in any age, can only operate within a broader environment which

• *adequate leisure time*	—long enough blocks of time at suitable periods
• *sufficient money*	—sufficient 'disposable' income
• *need or motivation*	—the desire or need to participate in tourism
• *freedom of movement*	—political and personal freedom to travel
• *necessary infrastructure*	—tourism infrastructure: means and modes of travel, accommodation, etc.

Fig. 1.1 : Tourism's enabling factors.

embraces a number of important cultural, social, geographical, economic, political and economic conditions' (Towner 1994 :7). Figure 1.1 summarises these tourism 'enabling factors' which, as will become evident, have underpinned the democratisation of tourism.

In the seventeenth century, of course, few if any of these factors had come to the fore. Nevertheless, two forms of tourism were prevalent during this period, both of which were influential in changing both the style and meaning of tourism. These two forms of tourism were :

- The Grand Tour
- Spa Tourism

The Grand Tour

By the late 1500s and early 1600s, the religious conviction that had motivated the pilgrimages of the Middle Ages was being replaced by more secular approach to travel, in particular travel for the purpose of education, self-improvement and, to a lesser extent, pleasure. More specifically, by the start of the seventeenth century it had become customary for the English aristocracy to send their sons, once they had graduated from university, on a tour of Europe. Usually accompanied by a tutor, the young aristocrat would undertake a 'Grand Tour' for a period of anything up to three or four years, visiting major cities, enrolling on courses at universities and learning not only academic subjects and languages but also social refinements. In a sense, Europe become a large 'finishing school' for young Englishmen, preparing them for careers as diplomats or in government. By the mid-1700s, an estimated 20,000 such 'Grand Tourists' were abroad at any one time, travelling through France, Switzerland and Germany, with the northern Italian cities of Turin, Verona and Venice featuring in most tours.

The Grand Tour is described in detail elsewhere (Towner 1985). However, the important point here is that over time, the characteristics of both the Grand Tour and those who undertook it changed. In particular, greater number of tourists started to tour on the Continent, but their trips tended to be shorter both in distance and duration and the focus of the trip became pleasure rather than education. At the same time, the tourists themselves came increasingly from the professional middle classes rather than the aristocracy. In short, the Grand Tour became popularised and, in a sense, moved 'downmarket' as tourists began to gain a reputation for showing little or no interest in the people, language or culture of the countries through which they passed.

By the late 1700s, then, the Grand Tour had been abandoned by the aristocrats who, setting a trend that has been repeated throughout the history of tourism, sought more socially exclusive resorts or destinations elsewhere (only, as we shall see, to once again be 'invaded' by the masses). The meaning or purpose of tourism had also changed from a cultural to a leisure activity; proactive learning and discourse had been replaced with passive sightseeing.

In particular, and reflecting the emergence of the romantic movement, nature, landscape and scenic beauty became the object of the tourists' gaze in a process perhaps best epitomised by the popularity of the English Lake District. Inspired by writers, artists, and poets, such as William Wordsworth, increasing numbers of visitors visited the Lake District from the 1750s onwards to gaze upon the landscape that represented the romantic antithesis to the rapid urbanisation and industrialisation of eighteenth and nineteenth century Britain. Thus, by the late 1700, travelling for pleasure or escape had emerged as an element of the tourism experience although still only a relatively small proportion of the population could actually participate in tourism.

Spa Tourism

At the same time that the Grand Tour was becoming a popular form of touring amongst the aristocracy, the spa towns of England and Europe were once again becoming popular destinations for the first time since their heyday in Roman times. In fact, spa tourism at this time represented the first example of resort based tourism and, similar to the development of seaside resorts a century or so later, the renewed interest in the spas was initially based on the perceived health benefits of 'taking the waters'. Bath, in particular, became internationally renowned, largely as a result of a book published by William Turner in 1562 which drew attention to the alleged medicinal properties of its waters. However, a large number of other spas were established across England (see Figure 1.2), whilst the fashion also spread into Europe with spas in France, Germany and Italy being redeveloped to cater for increasing demand.

Fig. 1.2 : Spa Towns in England and Wales.

It was not long, however, before the spas resorts were transformed from health resorts into social centres as medicinal considerations became subordinated to 'seeing and being seen'. In other words, visiting spas became an annual event on the social calendars of the upper classes, with Bath reaching the height of its popularity by the beginning of the eighteenth century. As more and more facilities were provided to entertain visitors they became, in effect, holiday resorts disguised as health centres and perhaps inevitably, they also began to attract increasing numbers of visitors from the expanding middle classes wishing to emulate the traditional clientele of the spas. Gradually, their social exclusivity began to suffer and, as retailers, innkeepers and a variety of other trades moved in to satisfy the needs of visitors, the spa resorts were being transformed into residential and commercial centres. Indeed, by the late 1700s their popularity had diminished significantly and tourists turned their attention to the new seaside resorts that, by the early 1800s, were becoming important tourist destinations.

Tourism in the 1800s

The nineteenth century is, undoubtedly, the most important period in the history of tourism. At the beginning of the century, tourism remained an activity enjoyed by a relatively small, privileged proportion of the population. For example, it is estimated that about 40,000 English citizens were either living or travelling in Europe at that time yet, by 1840, some 100,000 people were crossing the English Channel each year, a figure which had risen to one million by the start of the twentieth century (Young 1973). This rapid growth in tourism resulted from a number of influences, including :

- Technological advances, particularly the introduction and rapid development of the railway network;
- Increases in personal income, combined with greater amounts of free time;
- Social transformations that created the motivation for tourism;
- The foundation of the tourism industry.

Thus, although the greatest growth in tourism, manifested in the emergence of mass, international tourism, was to occur during the second half of the twentieth century, the foundations for such growth were laid during the nineteenth century. Of particular importance was the development of seaside resorts as the first step towards mass participation in tourism.

British Seaside Resorts

With the declining popularity of the spas during the late 1700s, the attention of tourists turned towards coastal resorts. Like the spas, the initial impetus was provided by the medical profession which extolled the supposed recuperative powers of seawater; a paper published by Dr. Richard Russell in 1753 described the alleged benefits of both bathing in and even drinking seawater and, in order to practice what he preached, he moved to Brighthelmstone (Brighton) on the south coast. By the turn of the century, Brighton had replaced Bath as the fashionable leisure centre outside London, its popularity boosted by a visit the resort by the Prince Regent in 1783, and the town expanded rapidly. Similarly, a number of northern coastal resorts, such as Blackpool, Southport and Scarborough, also grew in popularity, whilst resorts on the Kent coast, such as Margate, played host to increasing numbers of visitors from London.

Again like the spas, it was initially the upper classes that were attracted to the seaside resorts. Blackpool, for example, was described in the Blackburn Mail in 1795 as—

> the first watering place in the Kingdom, whether we consider the salubrity of the air, the beauty of the scenery, the excellence of the accommodation or the agreeable company of which it is the general resort.

This exclusivity was based on the initial health motivations for visiting the resorts—the experience was anything but pleasurable, with visits frequently made during the winter months!—and also on the difficulty of travelling there. Even at the beginning of the nineteenth century, the trip from London to Brighton could take two days and the cost of the journey was beyond the means of most people. However, by the latter part of the century many resorts had become, in effect mass tourism destinations.

The rise (and subsequent fall) of the seaside resorts is discussed at length in the literature (see, for example, Shaw and Williams 1997; Walton 1983, 2000; Walvin 1978). However, it is important to consider here the factors that gave rise to their popularity as tourist destinations and which, more generally, contributed to the growth and democratisation of tourism.

(a) Transport Technology

Although it was rail transport that as to be a defining factor, the Kent resorts along the Thames estuary were attracting an ever-widening range of social groups by the early 1800s, primarily as a result of the introduction of steamboat services. Sailing cargo ships had already carried passengers to resorts such as Margate but, by 1830, paddle steamers were carrying Londoners to the seaside in their thousands. In fact, the icons of British seaside resorts—their piers—were originally built for landing passengers rather than as places of entertainment.

Nevertheless, the evolution of the railways was to be as instrumental in the growth of tourism in the 1800s as was international air transport in the 1990s. The first rail journey took place between Liverpool and Manchester in 1829 (travelling at an average speed of 16 mph). By 1836 there were 700 miles of track in England and by 1848 this had expanded to over 5000 miles. The number of passengers using the railways also increased dramatically; by 1847, 51 million rail journeys were being made annually and the cost of rail travel fell rapidly. Thus, for the first time, cheap, safe and relatively fast transport (essential ingredients of the tourism product) were available. As a consequence, the seaside resorts expanded rapidly, with some, such as Rhyll in north Wales, owing their existence entirely to the building of the railways. It is also suggested that the social tone of resorts was, to an extent, dictated by when the railways reached the resorts and the distance from the main industrial centres. However, the development of the seaside resorts was a complex process and their degree of exclusivity cannot be explained by the expansion of the railways alone (Walton 2000). At the same time, it was not only the seaside that became popular—by the 1880s, rural areas such as the Lake District were also attracting significant numbers of tourists.

(b) Social Conditions

At the beginning of the nineteenth century, Britain was still largely a pre-industrial, rural society. About 80 per cent of the population lived and worked in the countryside and their leisure was determined primarily by custom and the agricultural calendar. By the end of the century, it was in the burgeoning industrial towns and cities that 80 per cent of people lived as the country passed experienced the Industrial Revolution. This rapid industrialisation and urbanisation of society created a number of condition for tourism to thrive.

In terms of wealth, average income per head quadrupled over the course of the century and so, although poverty remained widespread (mass participation in tourism amongst the working classes would not occur until the twentieth century), some working people were able to accumulate savings to pay for holidays. Indeed, some employers established savings clubs to encourage their workers to save for holidays. More time also became available for leisure. The working week/day was shortened during the 1800s and, for the first time, the Bank Holiday Act in 1871 provided workers with official holidays. Paid holidays would not be legally sanctioned until the 1930s but, nevertheless, the more enlightened employers offered their workers regular, official (though unpaid) holidays in order to improve productivity. Thus, 'wakes weeks', when factories, mills or even entire towns closed for a week's holiday, became commonplace in the industrial north.

Social conditions in the new industrial cities also created the desire to escape. Not only did increasing numbers of people take advantage of the travel opportunities offered by rail travel but cycling and rambling clubs were also formed, and the concept of the holiday camp emerged, as leisure became an important or essential element of social life.

Interestingly, whilst tourism within Britain was rapidly expanding during the nineteenth century, the upper classes, once again 'evicted' from their leisure spaces (the seaside resorts) by the arrival of the masses, sought exclusivity overseas. International rail services, such as the Orient Express, offered luxurious travel across Europe whilst the Mediterranean resorts along the French Côte d'Azur became popular amongst European aristocracy. For example, Queen Victoria and the Russian Czar both visited Cannes in the 1890s and, in real terms, the French Riviera was five times more expensive then than it was during the 1960s. This growth in international tourism was in no small measure aided by the emergence of an identifiable tourism industry, with Thomas Cook in particular playing a central role.

Thomas Cook

Although not the first to organise tourism commercially—Sir Roland Hill is accredited with 'inventing' excursion trains—it was Thomas Cook who was the first to fully exploit the opportunities offered by the new travel infrastructure. Indeed, it was Cook who, in effect, revolutionised tourism by transforming it from the preserve of the privileged into an international industry and, in the process, creating the package tour as one of the most popular forms of tourism. His success lay not only in his organisational abilities but, perhaps more importantly, also in his recognition that people simply did not know how to be tourists—they needed to be organised.

Thomas Cook's first organised trip was in 1841 when he took 570 travellers on a short, 11 mile journey from Leicester to Loughborough to attend a temperance meeting. Following its success, other trip were organised, motivated more by Cook's altruism than the desire for commercial success and soon he was running regular excursions. From 1848, tours were made in Scotland with up to 5000 tourists each season using Cook's services and, in the same year, he took a group to Belvoir castle. Although he first contemplated overseas tours in 1850, it was not until 1855 that his first overseas tour set off. This, however, ended in Calais owing to resistance from the French railway authorities!

Despite this initial setback, Cook's overseas tours became more successful and travelled further afield. His first tour to America was undertaken in 1866 and, once his son John Mason Cook (hence the initials of the present-day tour operator JMC) had joined him, the business went from strength to strength. Indeed, in some parts of the world, the company began to wield enormous power—for example, it controlled all passenger steamers on the River Nile from 1880 onwards and enjoyed a virtual monopoly on all tourism to and from India. In 1872, the first Cook's Circular Notes, forerunners to the modern traveller's cheque, were also issued. These were similar to the letters of credit used by travellers during the previous century but were much more flexible, being exchangeable at any bank or hotel involved in the scheme. That same year, Cook's first round-the-world tour was also organised.

Thomas Cook was not, of course, alone in organising tourism during the nineteenth century. Other now famous names also established tourism businesses, such as Sir Henry Lunn, who was organising skiing holidays in Switzerland by the 1880s, as well as a number of companies, including the Co-operative Holiday Association, that embraced educational and social aims in providing holiday opportunities. Collectively, they brought international tourism within the reach of the masses, removing the much of the mystique of overseas travel and providing standards and services that were affordable to a greater proportion of the population. Thus, by the late 1800s, the scene had been set for the dramatic expansion and democratisation of tourism in the twentieth century.

Tourism in the Twentieth Century

In the early 1900s, the development of tourism continued along the course that had been set during the previous century. The upper classes spent the summers in the south of France (it was on the Riviera during the 1920s that sunbathing first became fashionable) and increasing numbers of tourists travelled overseas. Yet, for the majority of British people, tourism was primarily domestic (at the seaside) and would remain so until the 1960s and 1970s. Nevertheless, international tourism in general was on the increase. Large numbers of Americans crossed the Atlantic and, prior to the outbreak of the First World War, up to 150,000 American tourists visited Europe each year. Travel was becoming increasingly comfortable and easy, no passports were required in Europe and consequently, many countries were becoming increasingly reliant on tourism as a source of income.

During the first half of the twentieth century, then, the pattern of tourism remained relatively unchanged, although ever increasing numbers of people were able to enjoy the benefits of tourism. Not surprisingly, the same three factors of time, income and technology were most influential. Certainly, levels of disposable income continued to increase but, from the late 1930s onwards, the amount of time available for holidays, in the form of holidays with pay, increased significantly for the majority of the population. At the same time, other factors influenced holiday activity :

- *Holidays with Pay*—in the 1920s, some 17 per cent of workers benefited from holidays with pay, though usually at the discretion of their employers. However, following the 1938 Holidays with Pay Act, paid holidays became available to most workers. By 1969, 97 per cent of workers enjoyed two week paid holiday; by 1988, 99 per cent enjoyed four weeks.

- *Car ownership*—in 1919, there were 109,000 cars on the road in Britain, a figure which had risen to 2 million by the outbreak of the Second World War. Thus, although international travel was beyond the means of most people, many were no longer dependent on public transport. Motoring became a popular form of leisure, opening up newer destinations and leading to the eventual decline in the railways.

- *Holiday camps*—holiday camps had existed since the late 1890s and, by 1939, over one and a half million people in Britain spent their holidays under canvas and in camps of all kinds (Ward and Hardy 1986). However, the 'holiday camp' is, perhaps, most widely associated with Billy Butlin who, after opening up his first camp in Skegness in 1936, went on to build a holiday business that remained popular through to the 1960s. By 1948, it was estimated that one in twenty holiday makers stayed at a Butlin's camp each year and, generally, holiday camps were important inasmuch as they established the concept of mass, organised holidays for people to whom paid holidays and free time were a relatively novel experience. As a result, people were prepared to take advantage of the revolution that was to occur in tourism from the 1960s, manifested in the emergence of international mass tourism.

The Development of Mass Tourism

The last forty years or so have, without a doubt, been the most significant in the history of tourism. The foundations of modern tourism were undoubtedly built in the preceding century, whilst the pattern of tourism development, whereby the fashion or trend is set by the upper classes or élite, only to be emulated by the middle classes, has been in evidence since the Grand Tour and continues to this day. For example, once exclusive destinations, such as the Caribbean, are now included in package tour brochures and cruising, again a previously up-market activity, has also been packaged.

However, recent decades have not only witnessed not only the explosion of mass international tourism in terms of numbers of tourists, but also its transformation from a luxury enjoyed by a privileged minority into an activity enjoyed by a large majority of the population (at least in the wealthier, industrialised countries). That is, it has become an accepted, or even expected, part of people's lives, a necessity rather than a luxury, a mass social activity that many consider their right to enjoy. In short, tourism has, since the 1960s, become democratised.

This remarkable and rapid growth in tourism has resulted from the same three factors that have enabled the development of tourism throughout history. Working hours continue to fall, though not to the same extent in different countries. Europeans, for example, tend to have longer paid holidays that Americans, although on average the British work longer hours than their colleagues on the continent. More flexible working practices have also contributed to greater amounts of time available for leisure activities whilst many people now retire early. Collectively, these trends have resulted in not only more people taking holidays out also, and more importantly, individuals taking more holidays. Thus, although the proportion of people in the UK taking holidays (of 4 days or more) has remained unchanged for three decades, the number taking two or more holidays a year has rose from 15 per cent to 25 per cent of the population between 1971 and 1998 (ONT 2001).

Similarly, income has increased significantly, allowing people to take advantage of the free time that has become more available and to spend a greater proportion on tourism. Between 1950 and 1980, for example, real wages for men doubled and, between 1971 and 1999, the amount spent by British tourists abroad increased sixfold in real terms (ONT 2001).

However, the most significant influence on the emergence of mass international tourism has been advances in air transport technology which, in turn, has underpinned the development of a sophisticated tourism industry. Following the end of the Second World War, large numbers of surplus aircraft became available. This, combined with the introduction of jet airliners in the 1950s, set the scene for the rapid expansion of commercial air transport in general and charter air travel in particular (See Holloway 1998 : 32–35). As the large airlines bought new jets, smaller charter companies could buy cheap, second-hand aircraft to fly tourists to their holiday destinations and, taking advantage of economies of scale, the cost of international air travel fell dramatically. Subsequent advances in air transport, including the introduction of wide-bodied jets and the latest generation of efficient airliners, have continued to make air travel relatively cheaper, thus encouraging the continuing expansion of international travel.

The first person to operate a charter holiday flight was Vladimir Raitz who, in 1950, organised a trial trip to Corsica. He went on to build his business under the name of Horizon Holidays (later to be bought out by Thomson Holidays) and, following his

lead, a large number of tour operators were established both in Britain and abroad. Since then, the package tourism industry has become increasingly sophisticated and diversified, whilst the scale of operations has increased enormously.

Transport	Technological improvement:	– wide bodied jets – more efficient aircraft – alternative (e.g.: high speed trains)
	diversification:	– charter operations – 'no-frills' flights
Accommodation	Innovation in accommodation services:	– time share/club share – self-catering – all-inclusives
Emergence of travel operators	Tour operating and travel retailing:	– large operators providing the 'complete' experience – image of safety, reliability – widespread network of retailers
	Scale of operations:	– economies of scale/the package providing competitive prices
Integration	Vertical and horizontal integration:	– improved quality – economies of scale
Development of support services	Banks/currency:	– increasing ease of obtaining currency
	Insurance:	– variety of insurance and insurance providers
	Information:	– Travel/safety information (the Internet)
	Health:	– Improved health services
Public sector involvement	Government policies:	– positive policies to develop tourism
	Consumer protection:	– regulation (e.g. EU Package Travel Directive)
	National/local organisations:	– services for tourists
Changing demand	Holidays:	– demands for new destinations, experiences etc.
	International business:	– growth in global business related travel
	VFR markets:	– new VFR markets related to global migration patterns

Fig. 1.3 : Factors influencing the development of international tourism.

The important point here however, is that the emergence of a complex and sophisticated tourism production system has been a dominant factor in the growth of mass tourism. In other words, although the same factors throughout history (time money/ technology) have enabled more and more people to participate in tourism, the driving force that has created the modern global phenomenon of international tourism has been the development of the tourism industry and its related sectors, as well as changes in the demand for tourism. These are summarised in Figure 1.3.

Conclusions

In a sense, Figure 1.3 represents the agenda for the remainder of this book. In other words, we are concerned here primarily with the business of tourism, the system of tourism production that enables millions of people to participate in tourism and which, as this chapter has suggested, has been a major influence in the emergence of tourism as a modern, world-wide phenomenon.

More generally, however, the history of tourism has been characterised by two trends which, to this day, remain evident in the evolution of tourism. Firstly, tourism has followed a pattern of democratisation, also known as the aristocratic model of tourism development, whereby the fashion has been set by the élite who are then emulated by the masses. This is, of course, inevitable in many forms of consumption. However, it has been a particular feature of tourism and continues to this day—the first space tourist who bought a 'holiday' on the international space station in 2001 is evidence of this.

Secondly, a variety of enabling factors have, throughout time, underpinned the growth and democratisation of tourism. In particular, technological innovation, increases in time and wealth and, latterly, the emergence of the tourism industry have all been major influences. Nevertheless, this remains only part of the story. Tourism would not have become the mass phenomenon that it is today, so it is important to consider the factors that influence the demand for tourism.

2

Tourism : Definitions and Concepts

Introduction

Tourism is frequently and justifiably described as a major phenomenon of modern times. The number of international tourist arrivals has grown spectacularly, from just 25 million in 1950 to over 664 million by the end of the last century, representing an annual growth rate of 7 per cent (WTO 2000). Receipts from international tourism have also increased remarkably—in 1950, international tourism generated US$2.1 billion, a figure which had risen to US$455 billion by 1999. At the same time, tourism has also spread dramatically, to the extent that few, if any, countries are not now tourism destinations. In 1950, just 15 countries accounted for almost all international arrivals but, by 1999, more than 70 countries attracted over one million arrivals, whilst even remote areas, such as Antarctica, now attract significant numbers of tourists each year.

However, these figures alone do not define what tourism is all about: despite its scale, scope and value and its global presence, tourism still means different things to different people. To many, of course, tourism is synonymous with holiday-taking, a time to escape and relax, whilst for those who work in the multitude of businesses that enable others to be tourists, it is their job and livelihood.

The purpose of this chapter, therefore, is to explore the meaning and scope of tourism as an essential foundation to the subsequent chapters in this book. In so doing, it will highlight the fact that tourism is essentially a social activity which involves millions of individuals travelling either within their own country or overseas. At the same time, however, tourism is big business. That is, most destinations do not welcome tourists for philanthropic reasons. Rather, tourism is developed primarily for its potential contribution, through tourists' expenditure, to local and national economies whilst, in both destinations and tourism generating countries, a vast and diverse array of organisations and businesses enable and facilitate people's participation in tourism.

In short, the driving force behind the development and promotion of tourism is economic gain through the profitable satisfaction of tourists' needs. It is, therefore, logical that the study of tourism should focus, as this book does, on tourism as a business. The first question to ask, however, is why study tourism in the first place?

Why Study Tourism?

Tourism has been the subject of academic interest for well over fifty years, although it is only more recently that it has been offered as a specific course of study. As a relatively new subject area it suffers a number of weaknesses, such as a lack of definitional consensus or formal theoretical underpinning enjoyed by other, more traditional disciplines (see Cooper *et al* 1998: 3), yet there is no denying its popularity amongst students. At the same time, as academics from a variety of disciplinary backgrounds increasingly contribute to knowledge and understanding of tourism, the subject is gaining increasing academic credibility. Nevertheless, the reason for studying tourism remains the subject of intense debate.

On the one hand, it can be argued that the study of tourism is primarily vocational; that is, it prepares students for careers in travel and tourism. To an extent, this is indeed the case, as significant numbers of tourism students subsequently secure jobs within the industry. On the other hand, there is also a variety of reasons why tourism is deserving of academic study in its own right:

- It is a major social phenomenon, the largest peacetime movement of people within and between countries that the world has known. The study of tourism provides an understanding of the nature of this movement, what drives it, and its consequences.

- Tourism has significant economic, environmental, social and cultural consequences for destination areas and communities. Whilst a recognition of these consequences contributes to the more effective management of tourism, it also contextualises the role of tourism in broader social and economic change and development at the national and international level.
- Tourism is often claimed to be the world's largest industry. Although its identity as an 'industry' is debatable (see below), there is no doubting the significant contribution tourism makes to the global economy and its interdependence with other economic sectors.
- Tourism provides a focus for an enormous variety of issues, whether environmental, political, social economic, legal, or cultural, and is relevant to the challenges of planning and development, effective business management, and governance. In other words, tourism is, in a sense, woven into the fabric of national and global economic, political and social systems and, therefore, provides a valid basis for the study of those systems.

More generally, of course, as tourism has become increasingly 'democratised', or available to the masses, it has become part of most people's lives. Therefore, it could also be argued that an activity of such prevalence, as well as the industry that supports and enables it, is deserving of academic study.

Definitions of Tourism

Such has been the growth and spread of tourism over the last fifty years that it is now 'so widespread and ubiquitous. . . that there are scarcely people left in the world who would not recognise a tourist immediately' (Cohen 1974). However, recognising someone as a tourist and defining who or what a tourist, or tourism, is are different matters and, given the rather abstract nature of the concept of tourism (Burns and Holden 1995), it is not surprising that there are varying and numerous definitions.

As a starting point, Chambers English Dictionary (1988) refers to tourism as 'the activities of tourists and those who cater for them', a tourist being someone who simply 'makes a tour. . . a sightseeing traveller or a sportsman'. More usefully, perhaps, the Oxford Concise Dictionary (2000) suggests that tourism is:

> *the organisation and operation of (especially foreign) holidays. . . as a commercial enterprise*

whilst a tourist is defined as :

> *a person making a visit or tour as a holiday; a traveller, especially abroad.*

In both cases, a distinction is made between the tourist as, implicitly, someone on holiday, and tourism as the process or industry that enables people to be tourists. However, neither fully embraces the true scope and meaning of tourism as either a social activity or a business, whilst the specificity of the definitions leaves many questions unanswered. For example, tourism implicitly involves travel (although it can be argued that 'armchair travel'—that is, watching travel programmes on television or reading a travel book—is a legitimate form of tourism), but how far does a person have to travel to be a tourist? Does travel have to be international, and for how long? Is a traveller always a tourist? Does tourism always necessarily require the involvement of commercial organisations?

As we shall see shortly, a number of definitions have been proposed that attempt to address these and other questions. However, the dictionary definitions cited above undoubtedly reflect the most widely held (though not necessarily accurate) perception that tourism is, essentially, the process or activity of holiday-making. Therefore, an initial way of exploring what tourism involves is to consider it in the context of one of the most commonly used tools employed by the tourism industry, namely, the ubiquitous tourist brochure.

The Significance of the Brochure

Despite the advent of e-commerce and increasing popularity of the Internet, the tourist brochure remains the primary means through which tour operators sell holidays. At the same time, browsing through brochures is often an essential part of a tourist's holiday purchasing process; indeed, planning or anticipating the holiday is all part of the overall tourism experience. However, the brochure is more than a medium through which holidays are bought and sold, for it is indicative of the breadth and scope of tourism, particularly as a subject of study. Not only does it embrace the role of the tourist, epitomising what many consider to be the social activity of tourism, but it also points to the scale and complexity of the business of tourism. The contribution of the brochure to the understanding of tourism is summarised in Figure 2.1.

Significance	*Relevance to the understanding of tourism*
Travel	Brochures signify travel, usually overseas and usually by air, to places that are distant, different or exotic. Thus, tourism involves physical movement to a new place, bringing tourists into contact with people from different societies and cultures.
Escape/relaxation	Typically, the pictures in brochures imply that tourism enables people to escape, relax and have fun in destinations where the sun is always shining. Thus, tourism also involves mental/psychological movement to new places.
Expenditure	Tourism is an expenditure driven activity, as signified by prices quoted in brochures. Tourists often pay significant sums of money in the pursuit of tourism experiences; their expenditure contributes to the global economic value of tourism.
International	Most brochures sell holidays in a variety of countries, signifying that tourism is an international/global activity and business. It also points to the challenge of selling a product (a holiday) that is consumed in another country.
Sectoral	Brochures highlight the different elements of a package holiday—accommodation, transport (flights and transfers), entertainment, activities, refreshment, insurance, and so on. In short, tourism involves a diverse array of businesses which collectively produce the holiday.
Promotion	Brochures attempt to sell holidays profitably whilst satisfying the needs and perceptions of tourists. Thus, from the industry perspective, tourism is a commercial activity driven primarily by the need make a profit.
Legislation	The brochure content is regulated by law; both the operator and the tourist are bound by the contract made between them and, thus, tourism is a highly regulated business/activity.
Environment	Brochures display pristine environments, and the success of tourism is dependent on maintaining an attractive environment for tourists. Thus, tourism is an ecological phenomenon in that it impacts upon and interacts with its environment.

Fig. 2.1 : Brochures and the meaning of tourism.

Typically, brochures suggest that tourists are motivated by the desire to escape on holiday to places, usually by air, where they can unwind and relax, and that there is a complex, multifaceted industry which can satisfy their needs. However, whilst this is undoubtedly one aspect of tourism, it is not the only one. In other words, the 'tourism' epitomised by the tourist brochure exacerbates a number of myths about tourism which contribute, according to Cooper *et al* (1998: 2), to its unrealistic 'glamorous' image. In particular :

- Although it is international tourism that has the higher profile domestic tourism (people travelling in their own country) is more predominant. It has been estimated that, globally, the total number of domestic tourism trips is between six to ten times greater than the number of international trips.
- Although air travel is more 'glamorous', the great majority of tourist trips involve surface travel, particularly by car.
- Although staying away is frequently an integral element of a tourism experience, in many countries day trips account for a significant proportion of trips and spending. In the UK, for example, day visits generated £ 38 billion in 1999, almost 60 per cent of the total of £ 64 billion earned from all tourism that year.
- Although tourism is synonymous with leisure travel, many forms of tourism, such as business, are non-leisure related.

Already, then, tourism is evidently a much broader concept than is initially apparent. Nevertheless, a variety of definitions have attempted to embrace both the 'technical' aspects of tourism and it essence or meaning as a social activity.

Tourism Technical vs. *Conceptual Definitions*

There are two main groups or classifications of tourism definitions, often referred to as *technical* and *conceptual* definitions (Burkhart and Medlik 1981: 41–43).

(a) Technical Definitions

Technical definitions attempt to identify different categories of tourist (and non-tourists) and different tourism activities, principally for statistical or legislative purposes. In other words, they are primarily designed to set the criteria by which tourism activity can be measured and recorded. The first such definition, proposed by a group of statisticians at the League of Nations in 1937, defined a tourist simply as someone who travels for 24 hours or more outside their normal country of residence. This definition included those travelling on business in addition to travel for pleasure, health or other reasons, and also introduced the concept of the 'excursionist' as someone who stayed in a country for less than 24 hours (for example, someone on a cruise holiday). Domestic tourists, however, were not included in the definition.

A similar definition, though utilising the more general term 'visitor', was suggested in 1963 by the International Union of Official Travel Organisations (IUOTO), the precursor to the World Tourism Organisations (WTO). It states that a visitor is:

> any person visiting a country other than that in which he has his usual place of residence, for any reason other than following an occupation remunerated from within the country visited.

Within this definition, visitors are sub-categorised as either tourists, who stay overnight, or excursionists on day visits. Again, however, domestic tourism is overlooked, an omission which the Tourism Society in the UK attempted to rectify in its definition of tourism:

> Tourism is the temporary short-term movement of people to destinations outside the places where they normally live and work, and their activities during their stay at these destinations; it includes movement for all purposes, as well as day visits or excursions.

Although including domestic tourism, this definition is still problematic inasmuch as not only does it include virtually any activity as tourism as long as it includes travel, but also the home environment and the necessary distance to travel to qualify as a tourist are not clarified. Nevertheless, it does demonstrate how broad a definition must be in order to cover all aspects of tourism.

In an attempt to provide set criteria in order to standardise the statistical measurement of tourism (the premise being that global tourism can only be measured accurately if all countries work to identical parameters), the WTO has published recommendations for the collection of technical data on tourism (WTO/UNSTAT 1994). These set out a variety of conditions, including :

- Minimum and maximum lengths of stay—one night and one year respectively (with the exception of day visitors/ excursionists).
- Distance from the normal home environment—160 km.
- Purpose of visit categories. Most commonly, these include holidays, business, visiting friends and relatives (VFR) and 'other', although more specific purposes are also identified (see Figure 2.2) .

Importantly, it demonstrates that tourism embraces a much wider set of activities and purposes than the more traditional perception of tourism as a leisure activity allows for.

To be included in tourism statistics		*Not to be included in tourism statistics*
Category	Purpose	Category
Tourists	Holidays	Border workers
non-residents	business	Transit passengers
nationals resident abroad	health	Nomads
crew members	study	Refugees
	meetings/missions	Members of armed forces
Excursionists:	VFR	Diplomats
cruise passengers	religion	Temporary immigrants
day visitors	sport	Permanent immigrants
crews	others	

Fig. 2.2. : Technical definition of a tourist.

(b) Conceptual Definitions

In contrast to technical, measurement-based definitions, conceptual definitions attempt to convey the meaning of tourism from the point of view of the individual tourist. That is, they attempt to address the role or function of tourism as a particular element of social life. Thus, it has been suggested that a tourist is a 'temporarily leisured person who voluntarily visits a place for the purpose of experiencing a change' (Smith 1989:1). Similarly, Graburn (1983) proposes that tourism 'involves for the participants a separation from normal 'instrumental' life and the business of making a living, and offers entry into another kind of moral state in which mental, expressive and cultural needs come to the fore'. In both cases, the emphasis is very much placed on tourism as a leisure activity, in particular one which acts as a contrast or safety valve to the pressure of normal, everyday working life. This, of course, excludes many of the non-leisure purposes of tourism referred to in Figure 2.2 but is, perhaps, more in accordance with popularly held perceptions of tourism.

It is evident, then, that it is difficult, if not impossible, to propose a single, all-embracing definition of tourism. Essentially, it is a social activity, in that it involves the voluntary movement of people, with the following characteristics :

- It is normally considered a leisure activity, although for statistical purposes some forms of non-leisure travel, such as pilgrimage, or business travel are also recognised forms of tourism.
- It normally occurs outside the usual place of residence and work; that is, it is associated with a change of location and escape from the routine or ordinary.
- It is a short-term activity or condition; the intention is always to return home.
- It is socially patterned. That is, participation in tourism and the choice of holiday or trip is influenced by a tourist's socio-cultural and demographic characteristics, including age, wealth, education and gender.

Nevertheless, as already suggested, tourism as a social activity could not occur on the international scale that it does today without the support of the so-called tourism industry. Indeed, just as the dictionary definitions of tourism cited earlier in this chapter refer to tourism as the commercial organisation and operation of holidays, it is important to view the industry as an integral element of the modern phenomenon of tourism. In other words, tourism is as much about the businesses and organisations that facilitate tourism as it is about the activities of tourists themselves and, therefore the study of tourism should embrace both 'the study of man [sic] away from his usual habitat [and] of the industry which responds to his needs' (Jafari 1997). Therefore, having looked at definitions of tourism as a social activity, the following section considers tourism from an industry/business point of view.

The Business of Tourism

As pointed out earlier, tourism is big business; in fact, many would claim that tourism is the world's biggest business or industry. As we consider shortly, it is not perhaps appropriate to describe it as an 'industry' in its own right but, nevertheless, there is no doubting the global economic importance. International tourism receipts alone (that is, the total spending by tourists on overseas visits) amounted to US $ 455 billion in 1999 and, if current forecasts prove to be correct, that figure could rise to US $ 2 trillion by 2020 (WTO 1998). If international fare receipts (receipts related to passenger transport of residents of other countries) are added to the value of tourism receipts, then international tourism in 1999 was an export market worth some US $ 532 billion. (International tourism is an export, in that a country sells its 'product' to overseas customers in return for foreign exchange earnings. Uniquely, however, tourism is not physically exported—instead, tourists 'consume' the product—tourism services—in the country where it is produced).

As Table 2.1 shows, in 1999 international tourism was the world's most valuable export category, generating US $ 7 billion more than the second highest export category, namely, automotive products.

Table 2.1
Worldwide Export Earnings 1998

		US$ billion	*%*
	Total worldwide exports: goods and services	6,738	100.0
1.	Tourism: International tourism receipts	441	6.5
	International fare receipts	91	1.3
	Total tourism:	*532*	*7.9*
2.	Automotive products	525	7.8
3.	Chemicals	503	7.5
4.	Food	443	6.6
5.	Computers/office equipment	399	5.9
6.	Fuels	344	5.1
7.	Textiles/clothing	331	4.9
8.	Telecommunications equipment	283	4.2

Source : Adapted from WTO (2000).

However, international tourism is, of course, only part of the picture. If the value of all domestic tourism that occurs globally is added, then it has been estimated that tourism as a whole generates a staggering US $ 4,000 million, a figure which, according to the World Travel and Tourism Council (WTTC), could reach US $ 7,500 million by 2006. This would represent 11.4 per cent of global GDP. At the same time, it has been suggested that, by then, over 380 million people will directly and indirectly depend on tourism for employment.

Of course, such vast figures are, at best, only estimates—given the scale and diversity of tourism, the paucity of accurate statistics in many countries and the difficulty in defining what businesses actually contribute to tourism, it is unlikely that the true value of tourism worldwide could ever be calculated. Nevertheless, even at the national level the economic importance of tourism is evident. In the UK, for example, tourism makes a significant contribution to the national economy (see Table 2.1).

The value of the global tourism business is, therefore indisputable; the nature or structure of the business is, however, less clear. In other words, the myriad of businesses and organisations that collectively provide tourist services and enable people to participate in tourism is often referred to as the tourism industry, but the extent to which this is a valid description is debatable.

Table 2.2
Contribution of Tourism to the UK Economy

Total revenue from tourism	£ 64 billion
(of which : foreign exchange earnings)	*£ 12.5 billion*
Tourism : contribution to GDP	4%
Tourism : contribution to employment	7% of workforce
Tourism : tax contribution to economy	£ 1.5 billion

Tourism an Industry?

An industry is normally considered to be a single, clearly identifiable economic activity with particular production methods, recognisable chains of supply and specific products or outputs. Thus, for example, the oil industry embraces exploration, drilling, refining and the production of oil products, some of which are sold as end products, such as petrol, and others which are supplied as inputs to other industries. Similarly, the automobile industry is in the business of designing, manufacturing and selling cars, and is comprised of car manufactures such as Ford and General Motors, and the multitude of smaller businesses that supply products or parts to them.

In the case of tourism, the inputs, products, methods of production and chains of supply are much less clear (see Mill and Morrison 1998 : 1–8). For a start, there is no single, definable tourism 'product'. Tourists 'consume' a tourism experience, the nature of which is as much dependent on the activities of tourists themselves as it is on the tourism 'industry'—in many case, such as when driving to visit friends or relatives, tourists may not require any products or services provided by the industry. Secondly, tourist services are supplied by an enormous variety of businesses and organisations, many of which, such as airlines or accommodation, are industries in their own right. Thirdly, although some businesses, such as tour operating or travel retailing, are quite evidently directly involved in tourism, the relationship between other businesses or organisations and tourism is less clear. For example, financial institutions provide foreign currency services and insurance companies provide travel insurance, yet neither could be described as tourism businesses. Similarly, a publishing company may produce travel guides, but it would normally be considered to be in the publishing industry, not the tourism industry. In short, the boundary between tourism and non-tourism businesses is often blurred. Fourthly, a number of other organisations in the public sector, from locally run information centres to national tourism bodies, also play a role in the production of tourism, though often on a non-commercial basis. Finally, there is no single management structure within tourism. Unlike traditional industries where, for example, the management of a car manufacturer has overall control, there is no distinct chain of command in tourism and frequently the power lies not with 'producers', such as airlines or hotels, but with intermediaries, such as tour operators.

The important point here, however, is that although it is easy and convenient to refer to the tourism 'industry', in reality it cannot be described as such. Instead, it is best thought of as a production system, the structure and nature of which may vary in different contexts according to the differing relationship between its different elements. Moreover, to further complicate matters, this tourism production system is itself a constituent part of a broader system. That is, the production system (or tourism business) is but one element of a wider set of inter-related structures and processes that collectively have been referred to as the tourism system, a concept which, as the final section of this chapter now discusses, provides a useful framework for the study of tourism as a whole.

Tourism as a System

As has become evident throughout this chapter, tourism is a complex, multi-dimensional phenomenon that is difficult, if not impossible, to define. It is certainly a social phenomenon, in that tourism is manifested in the movement of millions of individuals, both within their own countries and internationally, for a variety of purposes. However, that movement of people would not, for the most part, occur without the services provided by the 'industry', or tourism production system. Together, tourists (the demand side of tourism) and the production system (the supply side of tourism) combine into what has been described as a 'functioning tourism system' (Gunn 1994), an interdependent and dynamic system where, ideally, demand is balanced by supply.

This functioning tourism system has, according to Leiper (1979), three geographical elements :

Tourism generating regions: the regions which stimulates tourism, and where much of the tourism production system (especially tour operators and travel retailers) is located.

(i) *Tourism destination regions*—the regions which attract tourists, which experience the consequences of tourism, and where primary elements of the production system (hotels, attractions, facilities) are located.

(ii) *Transit route region*—this is both a temporal region (the short time spent travelling between home and the destination) and places visited *en route*.

(iii) There are clear inter-dependencies throughout this functioning system. For example, tourism businesses in the destination are dependent upon generating region-based companies (tour operators, travel agencies, airlines) for a supply of customers; equally, tour operators require an adequate supply of hotels in the destination, tourists require appropriate attractions and facilities, generally, destinations must be able to satisfy the needs of tourists, needs which are created or influenced by their own, home environment.

More importantly, perhaps, this core tourism system is also subject to a variety of external factors which determines how it functions (Figure 2.3).

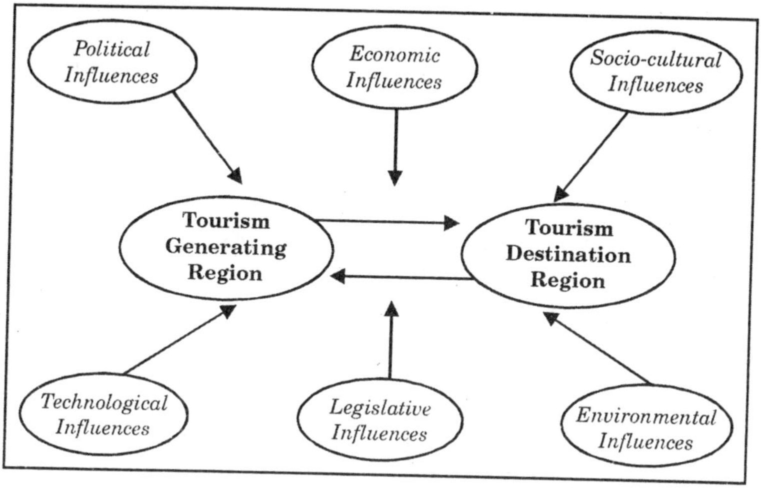

Fig. 2.3 : Tourism as a system.

These external factors not only add to the complexity of planning and managing tourism as a phenomenon that is related to national and international economic, political and socio-cultural structures, but also point to the enormous range of approaches to the study and understanding of tourism. Indeed, tourism is, perhaps, best defined as a social and economic phenomenon that cannot be divorced from the world within which it occurs.

Conclusions

In attempting to define and conceptualise tourism, this chapter has demonstrated the breadth and complexity of the phenomenon as a subject of study. Not only is tourism an activity participated in by millions of people every year, but it is supported and facilitated by an enormous and diverse industry, or production system. At the same time, tourism is both influenced by, and impacts upon, the environments within which it occurs.

Nevertheless, the fundamental feature of tourism is that it is, in a broad sense a global business; without the 'industry', people could not become tourists and, for most destinations, the *raison d'étre* of developing tourism is its expected economic benefits. Therefore, this book focuses primarily upon the business of tourism as, arguably, the linchpin of the global phenomenon of tourism.

3

Tourism Planning Approach of Malta

Tourism planning for the Republic of Malta represents an approach applied to an already established tourist destination. Planning is to shift the direction of the country's tourism development and to guide its future expansion.

Background

The Republic of Malta is an independent country located in the central Mediterranean Sea south of Sicily. The country is composed of the islands of Malta, Gozo and Comino and encompasses 316 square kilometres. The population is about 350,000, most of which is concentrated on the island of Malta. The country has a long history reflected in highly interesting archaeological sites, medieval villages, old town districts and buildings and extensive fortifications. The historic area around the Grand Harbour at the capital city of Valletta is particularly interesting. Malta is the home of the Knights of the Order of St. John. Some major historical battles were fought in Malta.

For tourism, Malta offers a mild Mediterranean climate combined with good beaches and scenic views. In addition to major archaeological and historic places, the traditional village and life styles are important cultural attractions. The country is conveniently located near to major tourist market countries in nearby Europe. Access for virtually all tourists is by air.

Malta already has considerable development of tourism. Tourism is mostly focused on Malta Island, but there is also some tourism on Gozo. The country received almost 900,000 tourist arrivals in 1990. Most accommodation is small scale, including many self-catering units, with only a few larger hotels developed. Tourist arrivals are heavily skewed toward the British market, and generally are low spending types of tourists. In the late 1980s, the tourism development issues were identified by the government as the need to increase income and employment from tourism. At the same time, it wished to improve the quality of tourism, including attracting higher spending tourists. The government also wanted to reduce the impact of high seasonality by expanding tourism during the shoulder and off-peak periods.

The Tourism Planning Approach

The Maltese Islands Tourism Development Plan was prepared in 1989 (UNDP and WTO 1989. *The Maltese Islands Tourism Development Plan*. Madrid: WTO). Although a separate project, the tourism plan was designed to be incorporated into the overall development plan and programme of the country. The overall planning was scheduled to be carried out subsequent to the tourism planning.

The tourism planning approach is a comprehensive one. The tourism development objectives are specified, based on the government's general objectives indicated above. A detailed environmental analysis was conducted. This is an especially important procedure because of Malta's small size and limited remaining natural areas. The environmental analysis identifies environmentally sensitive areas which should be preserved, as follows:

- *Agricultural*—lands of good agricultural capability that should be retained for agricultural use.
- *Ecological*—lands that contain important flora and fauna that should be preserved.
- *Geological*—areas of important geological features that should be preserved.
- *Entomological*—areas important as insect habitats.
- *Ornithological*—areas important as bird habitats, including stopover points for migratory birds.

Also identified is the location of underground water aquifers where any development permitted should have strict controls applied, so that ground water recharging capability is not impaired nor the ground water polluted. Because of limited water supply in the islands, maintenance of ground water resources is essential.

Existing land use is surveyed and mapped, using the categories of:

- *Development zone boundaries*—areas which are zoned and mostly already developed with urban uses. These areas generally would not be available for new tourism development (except urban tourism).
- *Industrial areas*—areas which have been industrially developed and therefore are not compatible with tourism development.
- *Airport*—the airport area is one where tourism development would be adversely affected because of aircraft movements and noise.

The tourist attractions are surveyed in detail and categorised, as follows:

- *Places of major historic interest*—these particularly include entire historic urban districts and archaeological sites.
- *Towers, forts and palaces*—these are specific historic features of touristic interest.
- *Traditional village cores and clusters*—these are village areas of traditional architectural character and lifestyles.
- *Major panoramic views*—the Maltese islands are small scale but hilly, and an interesting aspect of island tours are the many scenic views offered.
- *Beaches*—these are specifically located, named and classified into rocky or sandy types.

The approach to surveying tourist attractions includes identification and evaluation of the coastal bay resources for tourism. The existing areas of intensive tourism development were also surveyed and mapped in order to graphically show the relationships of existing development to the various attraction features. The location of existing tourism development is also, of course, a consideration in planning for expansion. This survey includes evaluation of the quality of existing tourism development, and its environmental integration as related to the beaches and coastal areas.

All types of transportation are surveyed and evaluated. First, the organisation of the transport sector is reviewed. Then, the major issues of air transport access to Malta are identified, with consideration given to travel facilitation procedures. The sea links to and among the islands are examined. Internal surface means of transportation, including bus, taxi and rent-a-car services, are evaluated. The short cruise boat tours offered by tour operators among the islands are also reviewed. Recommendations on improvement to all aspects of transportation are made in the plan.

All tourist accommodation is inventoried. A market analysis is conducted and market targets established based on the development objectives, evaluation of tourist attractions and other factors. These targets reflect the greater mix of types of tourist markets which the country wishes to attract and are realistic to accomplish. Based on the market targets, the number and type of future accommodation are projected. The institutional elements of tourism – organisational approaches and structures, investment incentives, legislation requirements and manpower planning– were investigated, with recommendations made for any improvements required. Economic, environmental and socio-cultural impacts are evaluated and recommendations made on these factors.

In preparing the plan, the major consideration was the need to improve and diversify the tourism product. This is necessary in order to upgrade and diversify the tourist markets, one of the plan objectives. Based on another plan objective, market and product improvements must be accomplished within the framework of expanding tourism as a major economic sector of the country.

For planning purposes, the two main islands of Malta and Gozo were divided into 12 zones, 10 on Malta and two on Gozo. This division provides for the systematic analysis of relatively homogeneous areas for which recommendations can be made. Within each zone, many recommendations are made on the specific policies that should be adopted and the actions that are required in order to improve the areas (as related to tourism development). TPUs (tourism planning units) are designated as specific no go' areas – places where no new tourism development should be allowed until detailed plans have been prepared and adopted to guide future development. Two of the tourism zones are designated as priority areas for improvements.

As part of the planning project, detailed planning and some urban design improvements were prepared for the two priority areas. Detailed planning, design and development programming were also prepared for visitor facilities at selected major archaeological and historic sites. In the implementation programme, the plan recommends an effective institutional approach for reviewing and taking action on future tourism development projects, such as hotels and resorts, proposed by the private sector. This procedure is essential so that new development projects reflect the plan's recommendations, and do not generate any environmental or social problems. Also it allows for efficient processing of the project proposals. The implementation approach includes a specific action and project development programme.

A major element of the planning study is the marketing plan and related product improvement programme. The market planning approach reflects the close relationship between developing the tourism product the promoting tourist markets. The strategy recommended in the marketing plan comprises the three elements of: (1) market diversification; (2) quality improvement; and (3) lengthening the tourist season. Then, derived from the strategy, marketing policies are determined and the action plans set forth for 1990–94. The action plans recommend specific actions and activities, related to coordinated product development and promotion, that should be carried out.

The product development programme specifies various actions for the short- and medium-term periods. These include the following :

- Implementing the tourism area upgrading schemes.
- Promoting hotel and other facilities upgrading with an incentive package.
- Encouraging the development of high quality hotels and other facilities related to specific target markets.
- Promoting the development of leisure facilities, such as yacht marinas, sports complexes, entertainment facilities, an underwater national park, cultural heritage sites, more shopping, and a light and laser harbour show.

The plan states that sufficient time will be required to achieve the shifting of markets and the product improvement needed, and that progress can best be made on a step-by-step basis. But it anticipates that, if the policies and programme are followed on schedule, the desired changes will be well underway by 1995. Over the longer term, the plan envisages Malta as a quality 'good value-for-money' destination, appealing to diversified middle and higher income market groups.

Conclusions

The Malta plan is a good example of a substantially developed tourist destination that needs to expand tourism for economic reasons. At the same time, the country wishes to shift its tourist markets to more diversified and higher spending ones. Another objective is to have better seasonal distribution of tourists throughout the year. A principle here is that, in addition to the greater expenditures of more tourists in total, the higher spending tourists visiting throughout the year will generate more income per tourist. The desired income will be generated by a fewer number of higher spending tourists rather than a larger number of lower spending tourists. This reduces the negative environmental and social impacts of large-scale tourism.

To accomplish these objectives, the plan recognises that the key issues are: (1) to improve and diversify (as well as expand) the tourism product of accommodation, other facilities and attraction features; and (2) to change the marketing strategy and promotion techniques. The plan rightfully emphasises that tourism product improvements and market changes must proceed together, as a basic principle of tourism development. The plan also recognises that these changes should take place within the framework of a comprehensive and specific physical plan, institutional improvements and development programming.

It is important to note that the planning includes a detailed environmental analysis which takes into account the scarce land and water resources of these small islands. This is an essential approach to achieve sustainable development. The land use patterns are also very important to understand in deciding on location of tourism areas. It is noteworthy that the tourism plan is intended to be integrated into the overall development plan of the islands. This should achieve better integration of tourism into the total development patterns of the country.

Dividing the country into tourism zones of relatively homogeneous areas represents an important planning principle. These zones provide a geographically rational basis for analysis and formulation of specific development policies, and for which to prepare detailed physical plans.

The marketing plan approach is a logical one that proceeds from general objectives to strategy, policies and action plans, with each policy and action plan specified in detail. Product development is carefully programmed and promotional techniques identified. In its statement that some time will be required to accomplish the desired changes, the plan presents a cautionary note to Malta that it needs to be patient but persistent in achieving its tourism objectives.

4

Tourist Attractions in the Oman Tourism

A detailed survey and evaluation of tourist attractions were conducted as a major element of preparing the national tourism plan for Oman. These provided an important basis for formulating the development strategy and programme.

Background

The Sultanate of Oman is located in the southeastern corner of the Arabian Peninsula. Its coastline of some 1,700 kilometres fronts on the Arabian Sea, and extension of the Indian Ocean, the Gulf of Oman and the Straits of Hormuz, which is the access to the Persian Gulf. The country encompasses a variety of geographical features of mountains, coastal plains and deserts. Summer temperatures can become very hot, including in the capital city of Muscat on the north coast. Summer temperatures are more moderate in the southern area, where the country's second major city of Salalah is located, because of a summer monsoon period. The average rainfall is light, but occasional heavy rains in the mountains can result in sudden flash floods that may cause considerable property damage. Oman contains about 1.5 million inhabitants, virtually all of whom are Ibadhi Moslems.

The country has a long and interesting history which provides many of its tourist attractions. There are numerous examples of settlements dating from the third millennium BC. Formerly known as Magan, the northern region has produced and exported copper, starting in about 2000 BC and continuing to the present. Frankincense has been produced and exported from the southern region since the first century AD. The Persians probably introduced the underground irrigation technique, known as the falaj system, in Oman in the fourth century BC. This system is still widely used in the country. Oman had a reputation of being a seafaring nation. There is evidence of trips being made to the Indian subcontinent from 1000 BC. During the seventeenth to nineteenth centuries, Oman became a colonial power and controlled Mombasa and Zanzibar—important trading centres in East Africa. During the twentieth century, the country's economy as based only on agriculture and fishing until oil was discovered in 1967. Oil production has significantly changed the economy and provided the resources for rapid economic development and rise of the people's income levels.

Until recently, international tourism was non-existent in Oman. Foreign visitors were allowed into the country only for business and related purposes. In 1987, the regulations were eased to permit holiday tourism to commence on a limited scale. Also, in that year, holiday visitors were allowed in without visas from the other GCC (Gulf Cooperation Council) countries. By 1990, 149,000 tourists of all types came to Oman, but the proportion of holiday tourists, excluding those from the GCC countries, is still quite small. The Gulf Coast tourists particularly like to visit the south during its relatively cool summer season. Oman has some excellent business-traveller oriented hotels in Muscat and Salalah, but tourist accommodation is limited elsewhere. Several tour operators and travel agents are established in the country. The national infrastructure is well developed and still being improved in the remote areas. Medical, educational and other services are being rapidly improved.

In order to diversify the economy and reduce the dependence on oil exports, Oman has decided to develop tourism on a very controlled basis. The focus of tourism should be on the country's inherent environmental and cultural attractions. The attitude toward developing tourism is a cautions one. Although the potential economic benefits of tourism are recognised, it is strongly felt by the government, and Omanis generally, that its growth must take place within a planned framework which seeks to safeguard the environment and protect cultural values. Mass tourism of the winter sun, sand and sea type is to be completely avoided. Tourism development that does take place will be carefully monitored to determine its environmental and socio-cultural effects.

Tourism Planning Approach

The tourism plan for Oman is a comprehensive one (UNDP and WTO, 1991. *National Plan for Tourism - Sultanate of Oman.* Madrid: WTO). It is based on specific objective, stated in the plan as follows:

- Develop a strategy for tourism which reflects the singular attractions of the Sultanate in relation to domestic and international markets.
- Base the strategy primarily on attractions of a cultural, environmental or scenic nature rather than on climatic or littoral (coastal) geography.
- Maximise the potential economic benefits of tourism within limits imposed by the need to protect cultural values and the environment.
- Provide opportunities for diversifying the economy and reducing regional economic disparities.

The plan examines all the components of tourism including the institutional elements. The market analysis includes tourist arrival targets established by five-year periods to 2005. These targets are broken down by holiday tourists of various types—international, Gulf expatriates and GCC citizens vacationing in Oman. The targets also specify various types of business travellers—international, Gulf expatriates, Gulf Arabs and Omani business. It is anticipated that business travellers will still greatly outnumber holiday tourists by 2005. Based on the market targets, accommodation needs are projected. Development opportunities and constraints are identified and alternative development scenarios are evaluated. The plan sets forth guidelines for formulating the preferred development strategy.

The tourism development concept is based on providing opportunities for informed tourists to experience the special cultural and environmental features of Oman. Six tourism zones are designated—three primary zones of attraction and three secondary zones. The major types of attractions are indicated for each zone. The plan also identifies several special interest themes based on flora, fauna and the country's history.

The plan recommends various tourist itineraries, circuits and excursions. A national itinerary refers to movement of tourists about the Sultanate as a whole. A typical national itinerary would consist of six to seven days in the north and three days in the south. A tourist circuit is defined as a circular route with a number of attractions along it. A circuit may take several days to cover and involve overnight stays at different places. Two such circuits are recommended. An excursion is a visit of a few hours or a full day to a place of interest, going out from and returning to an established base.

The plan makes recommendations on developing domestic tourism. These relate to the principal activities of domestic tourists and the supporting facilities required, and include beach park and recreation development.

A marketing strategy is proposed. This strategy emphasises image-building based on the country's cultural, historic and environmental attributes. Selective promotion would be directed toward the holiday target markets, and focus on both general interest and special interest themes. Assessments and recommendations are made in the plan on social, environmental and economic impacts.

Plan implementation considers several elements—organisation for tourism; procedural controls including licensing of suitable tour operators; manpower planning and training for tourism; promotional measures; planning actions including establishing a tourism information system; a detailed development programme; planning and pre-feasibility analysis of three demonstration projects; and outline local plans for two tourism areas.

Survey and Evaluation of Tourist Attractions

Because of the importance given to developing tourism based on the inherent environmental and cultural attractions of Oman, the survey and evaluation of tourist attractions are particularly detailed and specific. They are organised based on three categories of attractions—scenic beauty and environmental features; social and cultural attributes; and historic monuments.

A geographical analysis is made of the country's landscapes, including the mountains, coastal plains, deserts and the geographically transitional Muscat area. Within this context, areas of special scenic interest are identified, organised into the categories and evaluated as follows:

- *Upper wadis*—These are unique desert features of (mostly dry) streambeds, often within high rock walls, which can be travelled by footpath or road. The wadis are evaluated with respect to several factors–sense of enclosure; variation of views; frequency and variety of features of interest; interest of settlements; natural vegetation; water interest; and significance of end destination. Eleven wadis are designated as first grade attractions. The plan notes that some other remote wadis are likely to be at the same quality level.
- *Mountain areas*—Due to their accessibility and potential for providing recreational opportunities as well as outstanding views, three mountain areas are identified as having special touristic interest.
- *Scenic routes*—Scenic routes are defined as surfaced roads that offer visual enjoyment of the landscape. Scenic routes are evaluated based on several factors–dramatic scenery visible from the road; variety of interest; settlement character, special landscape features; density of vegetation; water interest; and length of scenic section. Based on this evaluation, eleven scenic routes are identified.
- *Beaches*—Tourist beaches are evaluated according to several criteria: fine light-coloured sand; a shallow gradient above the waterline; a regular gradient beneath the water permitting swimming within 15 metres of the shore; no off-shore current, undertow or fierce waves; sufficient length and depth to carry several groups in an uncrowded way; an attractive setting, preferably in a bay with a backdrop of hills; no incompatible development; a south/southwest orientation to maximise the number of hours of sunshine; and no conflict with sensitive environmental issues. The plan identifies eight first grade beaches and four second grade.

The plan examines the natural flora and fauna of Oman, and draws several conclusions. There is great diversity of birdlife, including migratory species stopping over in Oman on flights between Africa and India. Oman is internationally known as a breeding ground for marine turtles including four different species. The coastal waters support one of the best fisheries in the Indian Ocean. Major coral reefs lie offshore in several places. The plan indicates that Oman has been a leader in nature conservation, and that several nature reserves have been established. The plan evaluates and identifies the major environmental attractions related to flora and fauna which could form the basis of tourist itineraries and excursions, but under controlled conditions in order to protect the flora and fauna.

The plan indicates that the cultural roots of Oman lie in its historic towns and villages, and that these settlements are the focus for experiencing the culture and life styles of Omani people. Settlements are broadly classified into the three geographic groups—the communities of the coast, the mountains and inland desert plains. Each of these is examined in some detail. An inventory of these settlements was conducted and they are evaluated with respect to several factors—homogeneity of style or period; urban character; built form; setting; condition; general level of activity; special activities (such as festivals); and presence of exceptional buildings. Each of these criteria for evaluating settlements is assessed and assigned a one to five start rating. Based on the evaluation, the most culturally important settlements are identified, as follows—

- Settlements of the first order of attraction—10 places.
- Settlements of a high order of attraction—8 places.
- Other interesting settlements—10 places.
- High order attractions in ruinous condition—5 places.
- Settlements containing exceptional individual or groups of buildings—8 places.

The third major type of attraction examined in the plan is historic monuments. Archaeological and historic sites are reviewed with respect to their historic period—prehistoric (about 10000 to 3000 BC); Bronze Age (about 3000 to 1000 BC); Iron Age (about 1000 BC to AD 650); early Islamic (about AD 650 to 1650); and Imperial (about AD 1650 to 1850). The plan points out that some archaeological excavations and inventorying of sites have been carried out, but these are far from complete. In the plan, these sites are listed by area, described and classified as attractions according to three grades, as follows

- Grade A—Major site suitable for a visit of an hour or more.
- Grade B—Major site for less than an hour's visit.
- Grade C—Less important site with potential appeal.

There are many watch towers, forts, fortified houses and fortifications around towns, villages and entire palm tree plantations in Oman. Some 13 of these have been restored, and others are programmed for restoration. These are examined in the plan as a separate category, with the more important places specifically described. Other historic buildings and complexes of buildings are reviewed, including souks (traditional market places), mosques, falaj irrigation systems and aqueducts.

The survey and evaluation of tourist attractions are used as important input into formulating the tourism development strategy and programme. In addition, under the planning actions and policies section of the plan, general recommendations are made on the importance of conserving the urban fabric. Three categories of conservation of historic settlements are set forth in the plan—category 1 for restoration; category 2 for conservation; and category 3 for preservation. Policies are also recommended for managing the environment and inducing social and cultural harmony between tourists and the Omani host community. Detailed planning for demonstration projects include visitor and interpretation facilities at some priority attraction places.

Conclusions

The survey and evaluation of existing and potential tourist attraction features are given particular emphasis in the process of preparing the Oman tourism plan. This is because an important development objective is to base tourism on the inherent natural and cultural environment of the country, and to attract the types of general and special interest tourists who appreciate these features. Unless the attractions are thoroughly understood through survey and evaluation, it would not be possible to achieve the objective and prepare an appropriate plan. Also, the fact that there are a large number and diversity of both natural and cultural/historic attractions required that considerable attention be given to their survey and evaluation.

Because tourism is to be based on the inherent features of Oman, special types of attractions such as theme parks and casinos are not considered, as they might have been in some other tourist destinations. The approach used also reflects the development objective of not encouraging coastal tourism (the sun, sea and sand type of mass tourism). The survey and evaluation of beaches are related to development of recreation for domestic and Gulf Coast tourists, not for intensive use by international tourists.

The approach to survey and evaluation used in the plan is a thorough and systematic one. The attraction features are first categorised and then evaluated according to consistent grading systems. This grading provides an essential basis for deciding which attractions are the more important ones to recommended in the plan for conservation and development. Although the grading systems are obviously somewhat subjective, they do provide a meaningful basis for comparison when applied by experienced tourism planners.

An important approach used in this plan is to survey and evaluate the attractions within the context of researching and describing the overall geography of Oman and its cultural and historic development. This results in the planners (and users of the plan report) having a better understanding of the attraction features and being able to evaluate them more effectively. Serious tourists to the country will also have done some research and be knowledgeable about the geography, history and culture of the country. They will want to visit attractions that reflect this overall understanding.

Based on this survey and evaluation of attractions, the next step in the planning process was to select those attractions that will be integrated into the tourism development plan and programme. This involved other considerations such as access and location relative to tour itineraries and accommodation centres. Also conservation needs will be a consideration. For example, with respect to the attraction of marine turtles, utmost control of visitor viewing will be necessary during the season when they come ashore to lay eggs. When major attractions have been selected, they will require detailed planning for their conservation, development of visitor facilities and regulation of visitor use.

It is noteworthy that the government of Oman has established a highly progressive environmental conservation programme, with several nature reserves already designated. Coastal conservation management is also a major programme in Oman. Some restoration of historic monuments has already been carried out. This survey and evaluation of natural and cultural attractions, and the important role that these attractions play in tourism, may provide the impetus for continued and expanded conservation efforts.

5

Tourism Study of Goa

The tourism carrying capacity study of Goa, India, demonstrates application of carrying capacity analysis to several critical factors. This type of study provides important basic input to preparation of a tourism plan that is based on the concept of sustainable development.

Background

The state of Goa is located on the west-central coast of India, facing the Indian Ocean. Goa has a coastline of 106 kilometres of which about 65 kilometer consist of sandy beaches. The state contains a population of some 1.1 million inhabitants. Regional access is primarily *via* road and air from Bombay in the north. The local airport also handles international air traffic including charter flights organised for international tour groups. The state already has substantial tourism development. and attracted more than 900,000 tourists in 1988. The majority of these are domestic visitors but there are also many international tourists. Domestic tourists visit Goa throughout the year, with some decrease of arrivals during the monsoon (rainy) season. However, there is a definite seasonality of foreign tourist arrivals, with the low period during the monsoon season.

Most of the existing tourist accommodation is beach oriented and concentrated in the central part of the region. Some substantial new beach resort development has recently opened in the southern area.

The important tourism resources of Goa are the tropical climate, extensive beaches and a scenic natural environment of lush vegetation along the coast and forested inland hills and mountains. These inland areas also offer the opportunity for wildlife viewing. Significant attractions are associated with the region's distinctive cultural patterns of arts, crafts, music, dance, cuisine and highly interesting religious and historic places. Goa was a Portuguese colony for several centuries which left a cultural heritage that is unique in India. Old Goa with its sixteenth-century European style buildings and ruins is a major feature. More generally, the Goa architectural style of churches, houses and other buildings is of considerable interest to tourists.

The Carrying Capacity Study

The tourism carrying capacity study for Goa was conducted in 1989 (UNDP and WTO, 1989. *Tourism Carrying Capacity Study—Goa, India.* Madrid: WTO). This study also included an assessment of the social and environmental impacts of tourism and guidelines for the planning, development and control of tourism. The study was designed to provide input into preparation of a comprehensive regional tourism plan, to be undertaken in the early 1990s.

In formulating the carrying capacity study, it was first determined that the major attraction of Goa for holiday tourists is the quality and extent of beaches combined with the warm climate. This is reflected in the fact that, except for a few mountain lodges and facilities for religious pilgrims, virtually all existing and new accommodation development is located along the coast. Although tourists visit the natural, historic and cultural attractions located in the inland areas, they stay in beach accommodation and take day tours to the inland features. Therefore, the carrying capacities of beaches—alongwith labour supply capabilities, social impact evaluation and infrastructure capacities—are the primary considerations in the analysis.

The study estimates that an average density of 40 square metres of beach area per tourist bed would be an appropriate standard in assessing beach carrying capacity. This standard is, in part, based on the considerations of seasonality of tourist arrivals and the fact that domestic tourists do not make as intensive use of beaches as do foreign tourists. Domestic tourists spend much of their time shopping and visiting places. Assuming an average width of sandy beach of 40 metres, application of this density standard means that not more than one tourist bed per 1 metre of beach frontage should be developed.

Additionally, the study determines that not more than 70 per cent of the beach—or 46 out of the 65 kilometres of total beach length—should be developed. This factor is applied in order to :

- Protect the general landscape character of the area, with particular reference to the vegetation of coconut trees, as well as other aspects of distinguished coastal configuration.
- Protect the coastal villages, including several fishing villages, and their surrounding areas, so that villagers can continue their customary daily activities without disturbances.
- Avoid ribbon or continuous development along the coastline, but instead encourage development to take place in groupings with adequate open space and natural vegetation between these development groupings.
- Avoid disfigurement of the coastal character resulting from extensive building development.
- Cater also for the recreational and other needs of local inhabitants through development of public beach parks. These parks can be used by tourists as well as residents.

The standard of 1 metre of beach frontage per tourist bed is applied to the 46 kilometres of available beach. This results in an overall regional maximum development level of 46,000 tourist beds, or about 23,000 rooms.

Based on the existing configuration of accommodation development, the study estimates that about 30 per cent of beds of lower room rate level will be situated in places not directly facing the beach and sea, although they mostly will be within walking distance of the beach. Consequently, not more than 35 kilometres of beach frontage are expected to be actually utilised for development. This pattern will result in a density of about 57 square metres of beach area per tourist bed in accommodation fronting the beach. The study recognises, however, that some tourists staying in the nearby non-beach fronting hotels will also use the beach.

The study indicates that, because many domestic tourists do not use the beach intensively, it is unlikely that the number of people on particular beaches on any given day will exceed the established density levels. Even when a concentration of users occurs at the popular beaches on peak use days, the density will not likely drop below 10 square metres per beach user. This level is considered acceptable, both in this region and internationally.

Based on the 46,000 tourist bed figure, the study projects that some 4.1 million annual tourist arrivals could be received at the optimum development level. This is more than four and one-half times the 1988 level of tourists visiting the region. This estimate was determined based on three factors—reasonable assumptions of the ratio of domestic to international tourists; the average length of stay of each of these groups; and average accommodation occupancy rates.

The implications of the optimum level of development are calculated in the study. Based on assumptions of direct employee requirements of one employee per bed (two per room) in the higher quality hotels and 0.4 employees per bed (slightly less than one per room) in the lower quality units, there would be an accommodation employment demand for 28,000 persons. With the addition of employment required in other tourist facilities and services, 60,000 persons would be needed in direct tourism employment. Additionally, there would be generation of a substantial number of jobs indirectly related to tourism—in the tourism supplying sectors and the tourism induced economic activities.

Based on the present level of underemployment and unemployment and projected growth of the economy and population, the study determines that an adequate labour supply will exist to serve the projected level of tourism development, as well as other economic sectors. In fact, an important reason for expanding tourism is to provide more employment in the region.

The study evaluates the social impact of the projected level of tourism development. The approach used is to calculate the ratio of the peak daily number of tourists to the resident population within the tourism coastal development areas. This ratio was found to be well within the range of major tourism regions elsewhere in the world. Another important consideration is that the great majority of tourists to Goa are currently, and will continue to be, domestic visitors. These are people with similar cultural backgrounds and customs to Goans. Therefore, the ratio of foreigners to residents is much less than the overall ratio.

The future demand for water supply to serve the projected level of tourism is also reviewed. This is considered to be the most critical component of the infrastructure required for development in the region. Water demand is based on an assumed average consumption of 0.8 cubic metres per day per tourist bed, for a total of 36,800 cubic metres maximum demand generated by tourism. The study investigates the existing and proposed water development schemes, and determines that an adequate water supply would be available in the state to serve both tourism and general community needs. It recommends that water conservation techniques still be applied, including recycling of sewage effluent for use as irrigation water.

The study examines the other infrastructure requirements of the transportation system, electricity, sewage and solid waste disposal, and telecommunications. It determines that these will be adequate for the future level of tourism development, if infrastructure improvement programmes are undertaken as needed. The report notes current deficiencies that should be corrected in the near future.

The overall conclusion of the study report is that the main factor in deciding the optimum level of tourism development is the environmental carrying capacity of the coastal area of the region. All the other factors are more than capable of meeting the demands established by the environmental carrying capacity. However, substantial improvements will be required in infrastructure in order to both remedy present deficiencies and meet future demands. It recommends, therefore, that future development of tourism in Goa should not exceed 46,000 beds, including those in existing accommodation.

Conclusions

The Goa study represents a systematic approach to determining tourism carrying capacity. Several of the important types of measurement criteria are considered—environmental capacity for development and use without overcrowding, infrastructure; availability of sufficient labour supply; and social impact. Environmental capacity standards are established based on evaluation of the local physical environment, and the expectations of the types of tourists who now and will in the future be visiting the region. These are then compared to the standards which are applied in similar situations elsewhere in the world, to make certain that they are reasonable. The environmental capacity is focused on the capacity of the beaches to handle visitors. Although not specifically referred to in the report, the capacity of the adjacent lands for development of facilities was also considered and is, in fact, adequate for the proposed development.

An interesting and useful approach in establishing the coastal environmental capacity is first to remove from consideration those beach areas that should be preserved for non-tourism-types of development. This helps give greater assurance that those places will actually be preserved for other uses. If an adequate amount of beach area has been designated for tourism based on the capacity study, there will not then be the pressure for expansion of tourism development into those places that should be preserved for non-tourism uses.

Infrastructure is considered with respect to its adequacy in serving the existing development, and also how wall it will serve future development based on the proposed improvement programmes. This evaluation reveals that there is no problem in terms of basic infrastructure resources. The study, however, justifiably emphasises the need to remedy existing deficiencies and pursue expansion programmes as tourism grows.

The social impact evaluation rightfully takes into account that the majority of tourists are, and will continue to be, domestic ones with similar cultural backgrounds to residents. Based on that factor, and the projected low ratio of tourists to residents, the study concludes that there is not expected to be any serious negative socio-cultural impacts. The limiting of visitor density on the beaches and provision of public beach parks are important techniques to reduce any possible resentment by residents, due to a sense of overcrowding and loss of amenities because of tourism.

In preparing the regional tourism plan for Goa, the optimum regional level of development that is determined in the carrying capacity study will need to be properly distributed among the proposed tourism development areas. The carrying capacities of each specific development area should be calculated to ensure that the recommended types and extent of development do not exceed these local capacities. In addition to designating the tourism development areas according to logical criteria, the regional plan will need to take an integrated approach. Consideration will need to be given to the preservation of existing coastal village areas, expansion of coastal urban areas, location of public beach parks, and other types of non-tourism land uses.

There are not expected to be any serious adverse environmental and socio-cultural impacts from the expansion of tourism. However, the final plan will still need to consider application of specific environmental and socio-cultural control measures. This will give additional assurance that no problems will result from future development.

6

Tourism Development in Zanzibar

The tourism development policy of Zanzibar reflects a comprehensive approach to developing tourism, and it provides much of the basis for preparing the regional tourism plan. Related to the policy are the criteria established to select the tourism development areas designated in the plan.

Background

Zanzibar comprises the islands of Zanzibar and Pemba, situated off the coast of Tanzania in East Africa. The islands have a population of about half a million and constitute a semi-autonomous entity of Tanzania. The islands are well known for their production and export of cloves, which provide the major source of cash income. However, the government wishes to diversify the cash economy with the development of tourism.

Historically, Zanzibar was an important Arab trading centre for East Africa. It was a sultanate for many years prior to independence. Zanzibar also became a focus of Swahili cultural development. The Stone Town area of Zanzibar city is the largest and best example of Southern Arabian architectural styles and urban layout in East Africa. Stone Town and some palace and other ruins in the countryside are important historic attractions for tourists. Other attractions are the pleasant tropical climate, good beaches, marine areas for diving and sport fishing, scenic beauty, traditional Swahili villages and clove farms.

Prior to the mid-1980s, tourism development was very limited with only a modest level of facilities and services available to tourists. Attraction features required conservation and development and infrastructure needed improvements. Only a limited number of holiday tourists visited the islands. Since then, there has been some development of beach resorts and other tourism improvements carried out.

Tourism Development Policy

The Zanzibar regional tourism development plan was prepared in 1983 (UNDP and WTO, 1983. *Zanzibar Tourism Development Plan,* Madrid: WTO). The planning project was designed to prepare a comprehensive regional tourism development policy and structure plan, including the institutional elements. Detailed plans were prepared for specific priority development sites.

The tourism development policy recommended in the plan was quite comprehensive. This policy and its introductory statement, as extracted from the plan report, is as follows:

> Formulation and adoption of appropriate tourism policy is the essential first step in developing tourism. Tourism policy indicates the type and direction which the area wishes to take on tourism development and provides the general basis for planning tourism and making decisions on its continuing development. Adoption of tourism policy indicates that the area has made an official commitment to develop tourism, and the policy provides the legal basis for guiding the general type and extent of tourism to be developed.

The major elements of a suitable tourism policy statement for Zanzibar are recommended as follows :

- International tourism should be developed as an important means of achieving greater understanding and appreciation of Zanzibar's history, culture and natural environment by foreigners, and of residents, developing some understanding of other people's customs and cultures.
- International tourism also should be developed to provide additional employment, income and foreign exchange for Zanzibar, and to help diversify the islands' economy.
- Domestic tourism should be developed as an important means of recreation, increasing understanding by Zanzibaris of their own historical, cultural and environmental heritage, and by mainland Tanzanians of Zanzibar's rich historical and cultural heritage.

- Domestic tourism also should be developed as a means of redistributing income within Zanzibar, especially from urban to rural areas and from mainland Tanzania to Zanzibar.
- Tourism development should be integrated into the overall development policy, planning and strategy of Zanzibar, and receive appropriate priority and its necessary share of development resources.
- Tourism should be developed and operated so that it promotes conservation of archaeological sites and historic places, conservation and revitalisation of the desirable aspects of traditional cultural patterns, arts and handicrafts, and maintenance of the essence of religious beliefs and practices, all of which represent the historic and cultural heritage of Zanzibar. Tourism should be planned, developed and organised so that it does not result in serious social problems or cultural disruptions.
- Tourism should be developed in a carefully planned, controlled and organised manner so that it promotes conservation of the natural environment, especially places of scenic beauty, indigenous flora and fauna, important natural ecological systems, outdoor recreation potential, beaches and underwater environments. Tourism development should not result in any type of serious air, water, noise and visual pollution.
- Tourism development should proceed on a controlled, systematic basis, according to a staged programme of allocating development resources to specified places. The pace of tourism development should be kept in balance with the number and type of tourist arrivals, the development of infrastructure and with Zanzibar's economic and social capability of absorbing tourism growth.
- Tourism should be developed so that it will serve as a catalyst for increased development of related economic activities such as handicraft production, agriculture and fisheries and other related industries, and help in supporting improvements of transportation facilities and services and other infrastructure.

- Tourism should be planned and developed so that it makes maximum use of existing infrastructure, and that improved and new infrastructure should serve general purpose needs as well as tourism.
- Tourist accommodation and other facilities should be designed to reflect and represent Zanzibar's distinctive architectural styles, the islands' tropical environment and utilise local building materials to the extent possible. Maximum use should be made of renovated existing buildings which have architectural and historical significance for tourist facilities.
- All aspects of tourism development and operations should be organised so that tourism functions in an efficient and integrated manner to meet the needs of international and domestic tourists and achieve the objectives of tourism development. Especially important is the coordination of tourism development among the various government agencies and parastatals.
- Tourist facilities and services should be designed to meet the range of needs of various tourist market segments, including international and local standards, without being unduly expensive to develop, on the one hand, and always meeting minimum requirements of sanitation, safety and comfort on the other.
- Emphasis should be placed on employment of local persons in tourism. The persons working in all aspects of tourism should be properly trained to function effectively in their employment, and be given maximum opportunity for career development and job satisfaction.
- The general public should be educated to understand tourism and its role in Zanzibar's development policy, and be given all possible opportunities to use and enjoy tourist facilities and attractions while still respecting and maintaining suitable standards of these facilities and services.

The plan report recommends that this policy be carefully reviewed by the government, modified if needed, and incorporated into the proposed policy statement then being considered by the government. Alternatively, it should be adopted as part of the tourism plan.

Criteria for Selecting Tourism Development Areas

In determining the tourism development areas in the structure plan, several selection criteria are specified. These criteria are as follows:

- One or more important attractions within or near the area.
- Suitable and environmentally attractive sites for development of tourist accommodation (or existing buildings suitable for renovation), without creating undue social or environmental problems, for example, availability of sites which do not require substantial relocation of people or major economic activities.
- Adequate transportation access now or in the future to the area from the tourist entry points (airport and seaports) in Zanzibar and Pemba islands.
- Adequate transportation linkages to other development areas and to important tourist attractions elsewhere in Zanzibar.
- Availability of other infrastructure now or in the future, especially of adequate potable water, electric power, sanitary sewage disposal and telephone service.
- Availability or potential to develop the necessary other tourist facilities within the area (often these can be provided in the hotel or resort environment).
- Existing or proposed development of accommodation in the area—the existing patterns of tourism development.
- Interest of local residents in having tourism development in or near their area.
- Need in the general area for employment and economic activities.

Based on these criteria, several tourism development areas, mostly urban places and resorts areas, were selected and designated on the tourism structure plan.

Conclusions

The plan report first indicates why policy is important to formulate and adopt. This educates the government about the need for policy. The actual policy statement is comprehensive and refers to all the basic relevant themes of developing tourism. One theme is why international and domestic tourism should be developed, and both economic and social reasons are indicated. The importance of integrating tourism into overall development policy and patterns is emphasised. Another major theme is that tourism should be used as a technique for environmental and cultural conservation, and not generate socio-cultural or environmental problems. The approach to be taken of controlled, staged and integrated development is specified in the policy. Economically, the policy stresses that tourism should be a catalyst to overall economic development, as well as generating its own immediate benefits. The points are made that tourist facilities should be architecturally integrated into their cultural and natural environment, and make use of multi-purpose infrastructure.

Institutional elements are included in the policy. Reference is made to the need for effective organisation of tourism including coordination among the various government agencies and with the private sector. The importance of training and employing local residents is stressed. The need for public education about tourism is indicated. The point is made that residents should have access to tourist attractions and facilities. The concept of developing quality tourism that meets the expectations of tourists is set forth.

The criteria applied for selecting tourism development areas reflect a specific and systematic approach to preparing the structure plan. The selection criteria consider all the important physical factors—tourist attractions, environmental suitability, transportation access and linkages, availability of other infrastructure and existing development patterns. Socio-economic considerations, about the interest of local residents in developing tourism and local economic development needs, are also indicated. Not listed here, but also applied as a criterion in the plan, was that tourism should not pre-empt places or resources that are more important for other types of uses and development.

7

Tourism Planning in Bhutan

Policy and planning for tourism in Bhutan are based on the concept of maintaining high value, special interest and adventure tourism, which is developed in a very controlled and staged manner. There is much involvement of the government and religious leaders in the planning and management process.

Background

Located in the eastern Himalaya Mountains of South Asia, the Kingdom of Bhutan is mostly high and mountainous. Bordering India on the south are foothills with subtropical wildlife and vegetation. The country contains a population of about 1.5 million, most of which is agricultural. Only about 5 per cent of the people live in urban places. Nomadism is still practised by certain groups in the higher elevations. Many Bhutanese live a relatively secure and comfortable subsistence life style that is not, to a great extent, integrated into the modern cash economy.

Attractions for tourists are the spectacular mountain scenery and strongly traditional Buddhist cultural patterns. The distinctive Bhutanese architectural styles of monasteries, palaces, shops and homes are a major feature. The castle-monasteries called *dzongs* are particularly striking features of the cultural landscape. Handicrafts are available. Cultural tours and mountain trekking are the most popular activities of tourists. Access to the country for tourists is primarily by air to the international airport at Paro in western Bhutan. The airport is at a relatively short distance from the capital city of Thimpu, and connects to the country's road network. There is also one road access from India in the southwest.

Tourism in Bhutan commenced after the Royal Coronation of the present king in 1974, when it was realised that the hotels developed for that event could be utilised for tourists. The objectives of tourism at the time of its introduction were to:

- Generate revenue, especially foreign exchange.
- Publicise the culture and traditions of the country to the outside world.
- Play an active role in the country's socio-economic development.

However, the government was concerned that the unrestricted flow of tourists could lead to socio-cultural and environmental problems, and it applied a strict policy of controlling tourism development. Until the mid-1980s, the maximum number of international holiday tourist arrivals, excluding the neighbouring Indians, was maintained at 2,000 annually. In 1986, 2,500 arrivals were targeted. Arrivals have remained at about the 2,500–3,000 level into the early 1990s.

The Tourism Plan

A national tourism development plan was completed in 1984 and, after long debate by the government, adopted in 1986 (UNDP and WTO, 1986. *Tourism Development Master Plan for Bhutan.* Madrid: WTO). The plan indicates that Bhutan's resources present potential for three types of tourism, each in a different geographical zone, as follows:

- Himalayan zone for mountaineering and high altitude trekking.
- Central zone for cultural tours, including treeking.
- Southern foothills zone for wildlife tourism in conjunction with Indian winter tourism.

The plan states that, 'The central cultural zone has unique attractions by world standards, and creates great potential as a focus for all aspects of Bhutanese tourism development'.

The plan recognises the government's desire to continue the policy of controlled tourism development, gradually opening up new areas as infrastructure is developed. The overriding aim is to ensure that the type and rate of growth of tourism does not damage the natural environment nor degrade the cultural

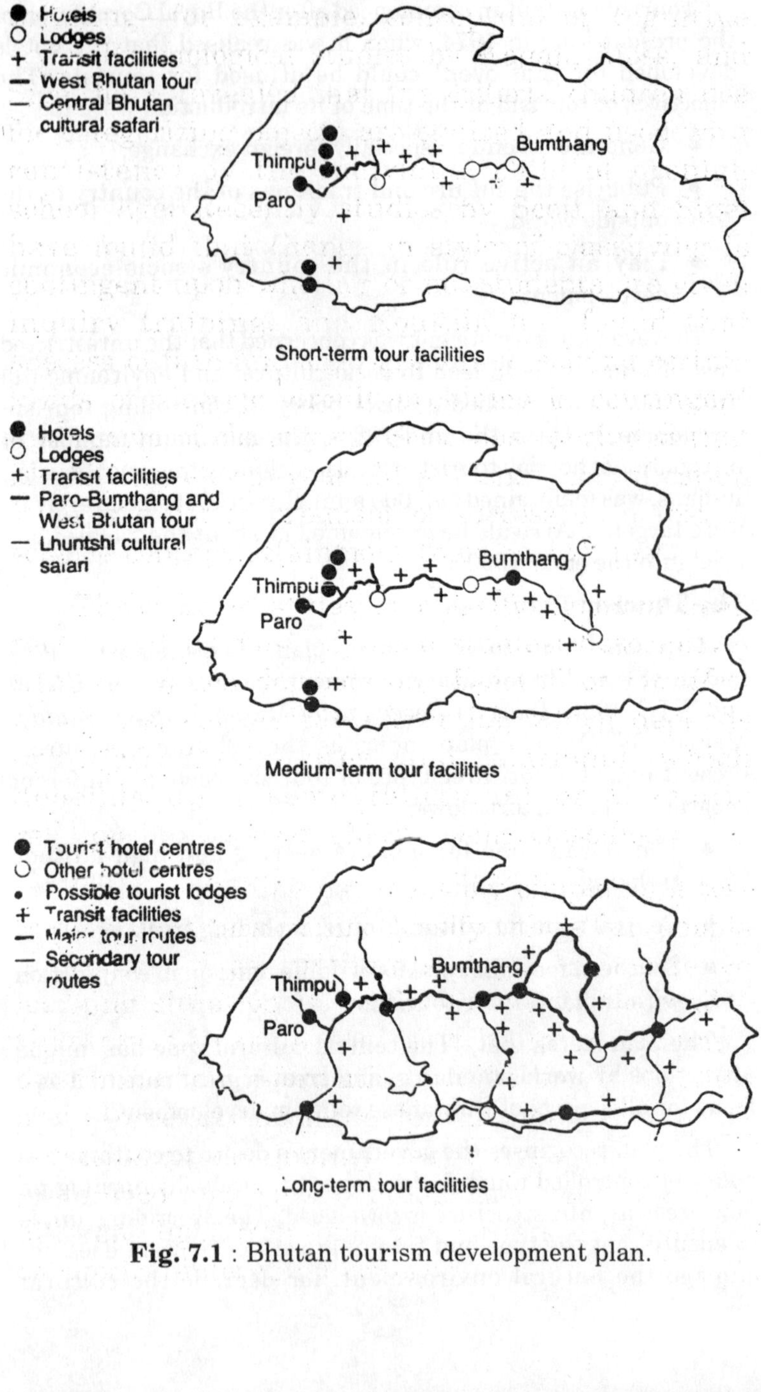

Fig. 7.1 : Bhutan tourism development plan.

heritage. In fact, the tourism plan views controlled tourism as an important vehicle for conserving and enhancing the cultural assets of the country.

In the tourism plan, growth targets for international tourist arrivals were set at 3,000 for 1990 and 5,600 for 1995 under the preferred strategy. The National Seventh Five-Year Development Plan for 1992–96 closely follows and further refines these market targets.

The tourism development strategy set forth in the plan is to focus development around tourism service centres in the main potential areas, liked by tourist excursion routes. Eight such centres are recommended for the long-term period in the western, central, eastern and southern regions of the country. The strategy identifies three time phases, which are illustrated in Figure 7.1, and described as follows :

- *Short-term (1986–90)*—Continuation of the process of improving standards of tourist facilities and services with high utilisation of existing infrastructure in the presently opened areas in the western and central regions.
- *Medium-term (1991–95)*—Expansion of tourism in the central region with development of some new facilities and infrastructure, and starting cultural safari tourism in the eastern region.
- *Long-term (post 1995)*—Further expansion of tourism development in the western and central regions, gradual expansion of development in the eastern region, and development of wildlife tourism in the southern region.

The plan reinforces that already established policy of the government that the architectural design of any new development, including tourist facilities, must utilise traditional design motifs and building materials to the greatest extent possible. This policy has been followed. Recently developed hotels and other buildings, especially in the rapidly growing capital city of Thimpu, incorporate the traditional architectural character and blend in well with older development and the natural environment.

Adequate sewage disposal systems for hotels are also required. Electric power is provided from the national grid in the more developed areas and on-site generation is used in other places.

More generally, the country has adopted a policy, and has programmes underway, for strict conservation of the natural environment.

In order to provide trained tourism personnel, a training unit was set up at the Bhutan Hotel in Thimpu in the mid-1980s under the UNDP/WTO. This project also included overseas education in hotel and tourism management for several persons.

In the mid-1980s, some religious leaders objected to certain forms of tourist activities, particularly those that involve tourists visiting important religious sites. A special tourism commission was established and it investigated the situation. The commission reported to the National Assembly that tourism may have an adverse moral impact on young people, if they observe tourists' behaviour that might be interpreted as belittling the mystical power of the country's religious beliefs. This resulted in a Royal Command to the tourism office to designate certain monasteries and temples closed to tourists, effective in 1988. This seems to have been an acceptable arrangement to the parties involved.

In order to carry out the concept of controlled, high value tourism, certain approaches have been applied. All non-Indian tourists must come on pre-arranged, all-inclusive package tours, and no individual tourists are permitted entry into the country. These package tourists must obtain visas before arrival. Presumably, if the planned number of tourist arrivals is going to be exceeded in a particular year, no more tour groups would be allowed in during that period. Also, marketing of tourism for the country is kept very limited and targeted to special interest groups, so as not to encourage casually interested tourists. Minimum daily expenditures per tourist have been established. These vary depending on the season and type of tour and are periodically increased. These required minimum expenditures are much higher than the average expenditures of tourists elsewhere in South Asia.

Contacts are maintained with overseas tour operators who specialise in Bhutan tours. These operators handle the visa arrangements and receive the tourists' tour payments before arrival in the country. Approximately 30 per cent of the tourists come for cultural tours and most of the remainder for trekking, including cultural treks to visit monasteries and historic places.

A very limited number of mountain climbing expeditions are allowed.

Conclusions

The Bhutan plan demonstrates the application of establishing tourism zones, in this case based on different geographical areas which are related to different types of tourist attractions and activities. The plan also applies the concept of establishing tourism centres. An important aspect of the plan is logical staging of development during successive five-year periods. Although specified by time periods, in fact, this staging can be carried out within a flexible time frame depending on future circumstances, especially development of infrastructure.

The plan reflects the strong government policy to control tourism so that any undesirable impacts on the natural and cultural environment are minimised. Controlling impacts is achieved primarily through limiting the number of tourist arrivals. In Bhutan, the limitation on tourist arrivals is maintained by requiring that all tourists come on package tours and obtain visas before arrival. This approach is in contrast to some countries which remove visa requirements, or allow visas to be given on arrival, to many types of tourists, in order to encourage more tourism. The package tours also provide the opportunity to control the travel movements of all tourists. In order to receive substantial economic benefits from tourism. Bhutan somewhat compensates for the limited number of tourists by requiring a high level of tourist expenditures.

As another controlled tourism technique, the limited and targeted marketing—as well as the high spending levels required—will tend to attract only those tourists who have a serious interest in, and respect for, the country's culture and environment. Impacts are also controlled and tourism development environmentally integrated by requiring compatible architectural styles of tourist facilities and proper development of infrastructure An important impact control measure is prohibition of entry of tourists to certain culturally sensitive religious monuments.

The tourism education and training programme and training unit were particularly important to develop in Bhutan because of the lack of tourism trained personnel in the country. This programme provides the skills and knowledge necessary to operate good quality tourist facilities and services, and to manage highly controlled development.

The approach in Bhutan includes the strong involvement of the government and religious leaders in the planning and management process. In this manner, the plan recommendations reflect government and religious policy, and the plan will receive good support. As should be done in any tourism area, continuous monitoring of tourism is maintained in Bhutan. When problems arise, as they did in 1987, the situation is investigated and remedial measures taken. Thus, tourism can be continuously responsive to local people's concerns while still generating benefits to the country.

8

Tourism Development in Bangladesh

The tourism development policy and strategy of Bangladesh represent a regionalisation approach to developing tourism. They are based on a realistic appraisal of the opportunities and constraints of developing tourism.

Background

Bangladesh is located in South Asia within the eastern part of India. The country contains somewhat more than 115 million people, most of whom live in densely settled rural and agricultural areas. The landscape of Bangladesh is dominated by the major river systems that flow through it—the Jamuna (Brahmaputra), Padma (Ganges) and Meghna Rivers. Most of the land is flat with some hills in the east and northeast. The two main cities are the capital of Dhaka in the central part of the country, and Chittagong, a major port in the eastern area. There are numerous towns scattered throughout the country.

The attractions for tourists relate to both natural and cultural features. There are major beaches at Cox's Bazar and the Teknaf Peninsula on the eastern coast, and elsewhere. A beach resort is already developed at Cox's Bazar. The Rangamati and Chittagong Hill Tracts, also in the east, offer scenic landscapes, indigenous tribal life and lake recreation. Some interesting forests, tea plantations and birdlife lie in the Sylhet district in the northeast. The Sunderbans in the south contain vast mangrove and tidal forest with ample wildlife including the Bengal tiger and crocodiles. More generally, the extensive river system offers opportunities for developing riverine tourism.

The country's historical heritage reflects various cultural influences. Dhaka contains a number of buildings from the Moghul and British periods, and has a national museum. A major historic palace in Dhaka has recently been restored and will be available for tourist use. Near to Dhaka, a major historic town heritage site has been developed. Of much archaeological and historic interest are some impressive Buddhist monuments dating from the third century BC at various inland sites. There are major Islamic monuments, and other places of historic importance. The popular culture of Bengali music, song and dance, religious festivals, arts, crafts and cuisine are all of considerable touristic interest.

Bangladesh has limited tourism development. There were 115,000 tourist arrivals in 1990, of which the majority were travellers on business, official mission or visiting friends and relatives. A substantial proportion of the arrivals are from India and other countries in South Asia, with most of the remainder from Europe and the Americas. The level of tourist arrivals fluctuates considerably from year to year, particularly depending on the incidence of natural disasters (flooding) experienced by the country. Slightly over 3,000 accommodation rooms were reported to exist in the country in 1990. There are two major international hotels situated in Dhaka.

Infrastructure for tourism is still limited, and access to some attraction areas can be difficult. However, there are two international airports—the main one at Dhaka and the other at Chittagong—and several regional airports within the country. Various areas are served by roads and railways, as well as by boats on the extensive river system. Because of the many wide rivers, river crossings are often by ferry boat.

The Bangladesh Parjatan Corporation (BPC), the national tourism organisation and a semi-autonomous body, is responsible for the marketing, regulation and several of the operational activities of tourism. The private sector is also involved in commercial tourism operations.

Tourism Development Policy

The tourism development plan for Bangladesh was prepared in 1988 (UNDP and WTO, 1988. *Strategic Master Plan for Tourism in Bangladesh.* Madrid: WTO). This is a comprehensive plan that examines and makes recommendations on all aspects of tourism. It gives consideration to both international and domestic tourism. In the plan, tourist attractions, facilities, services and infrastructure are described and evaluated. A detailed market analysis is presented of both international and domestic tourists. This analysis establishes market targets for the year 2000. The total target is 300,000 arrivals, with the majority from other South Asian countries, and lesser numbers from Europe, Southeast and East Asia, North America and elsewhere. About two-thirds of the arrivals are expected to be business-related. Domestic tourism is foreseen to expand rapidly. The plan reviews the institutional elements of tourism in detail. It also examines environmental, economic and socio-cultural considerations.

With respect to the objectives of developing tourism, the plan identifies several ways in which tourism can bring benefits to the country, as follows :

- Increased foreign exchange earnings to improve the balance of payments.
- Provision of income to people working in tourism.
- Increased employment in this generally labour-intensive industry.
- More intensive use of existing investments in airports, the national airline, transport and accommodation.
- Reaffirmation and development of local culture and national identity.
- Stimulation of the conservation of historic monuments and preservation of the remaining natural reserves.

The tourism development policy and strategy were formulated to respond to the principal economic, social and cultural objectives for tourism in the country. The important policies are summarised in the plan as follows :

- Pursue the gradual and controlled development of domestic and international tourism.
- Concentrate marketing resources on selected source markets and market segments, and integrate international marketing initiatives with those of other agencies and countries in the region.

- Establish zones of tourism development within which tourism investments could be consolidated and attractions clustered.
- Promote conservation and preservation of land, wildlife and cultural heritage.
- Develop an attractive tourism environment, through the relaxation of controls restricting entry into and travel within Bangladesh.
- Promote and foster culture and sport, and encourage participation from international and domestic visitors (particularly youth).
- Strengthen domestic inter-sectoral economic linkages; reduce the import content of tourism; and increase foreign exchange earnings.
- Strengthen and improve the tourism infrastructure including transportation.

The plan states that implementation of these policies entails provision of an appropriate framework within which tourism can develop.

Tourism Development Strategy

The tourism development strategy is based on the regionalisation approach of establishing tourism zones, each focused on a cluster of attractions. Each zone is based on different types of tourist attractions and related tourist activities, facilities and services. Figure 8.1 shows the six tourism zones which are designated in the plan. The Dhaka zone will also serve as the major international gateway and staging area for the country. As indicated in the figure, the major types of attractions, priority improvements required and time frame for development are specified for each zone. The plan states that development strategies should be centred on a unique tourism theme appropriate to each zone, such as the following—

- *River tourism*—This will capitalise on Bangladesh's many rivers and waterways, and can provide good access to various points of interest.
- *Village tourism*—This will complement the development of river tourism in many places. Several villages close to

Dhaka could be developed for day excursions from the capital. Village tourism can assist the local people in developing their communities.

- *Cultural heritage*—This has an important education element and can be divided into several categories—archaeological sites; historic monuments and buildings; museums; and fine and performing arts. Conservation is of utmost importance in developing cultural heritage tourism.
- *Forests and wildlife*—The development of this type of tourism should proceed in tandem with, and help justify, a preservation strategy for the country's forests and wildlife. This strategy has several components—upgrading the Dhaka zoo; increasing interpretation at selected sites; opening animal breeding stations to visitors; encouraging camping vacations and picnicking excursions; and introducing river tours in the Sunderbans forest and wildlife sanctuary.

In order to support the development of these types of tourism in the designated zones, the plan states that the strategy should seek to improve the tourism product. Product improvements should be aimed at accommodation, handicrafts, speciality shopping, nightclubs, urban-type products and sports. An important part of the strategy is to strengthen the institutional framework, and attract the required levels of investment needed in both the public and private sectors. The plan indicates that the public sector should take responsibility for tourism planning, provision of essential physical infrastructure and conservation, and protection of tourism's natural and cultural assets. The private sector should bear the responsibility for operation and management of commercial tourist facilities and services.

The plan examines ways to strengthen the organisational structures for tourism. It recommends that, toward the end of the planning period, a tourism development corporation be established. This would absorb the investment division of the BPC, and provide a vehicle to channel equity and local capital from the public sector to individual private sector enterprises.

To implement proper development within the designated tourism zones, the plan recommends a coordinated planning approach, as follows :

- Control and prohibit illegal and unplanned development in tourism areas.
- Safeguard the landscape and natural environment.
- Conserve the historic fabric of the country.

The plan recommends that there be close coordination among all the agencies responsible for the respective aspects of implementation. Town planning ordinances and powers should be extended to control development in the tourism zones. All forms of development within the zones should require planning permission and conform to the overall development plan. Institutional support should be given to the private sector, including provision of suitably serviced development sites within the tourism zones. The country's tax system should be structured to encourage investment in tourism, as well as generate government revenues. The strategy also aims at strengthening tourism links with the agricultural sector in order to increase local inputs of food items to tourism.

On marketing, the plan recommends short, medium– and longer-term strategies. For the short-term, marketing should be limited to domestic and South Asian source markets until some product improvements are made. During the medium-term, marketing should be directed particularly at attracting travellers from countries served by the expanded national airlines network. Other airlines and tour operators in the source market countries are also important in medium-term marketing. Over the longer-term, when product development has advanced, all the targeted markets can be promoted. Also, stopovers of multi-destination tourists in South Asia can be encouraged.

Based on the development strategy, a specific ten-year development programme, including project profiles, was prepared. Also development standards and architectural guidelines are recommended. Education and training for tourism are examined, with the conclusion that the present tourism training school programme is adequate to meet future needs.

Conclusions

The approach to preparing the tourism plan was a comprehensive one, with all the necessary elements of tourism considered. The emphasis was on a strategic approach. This is

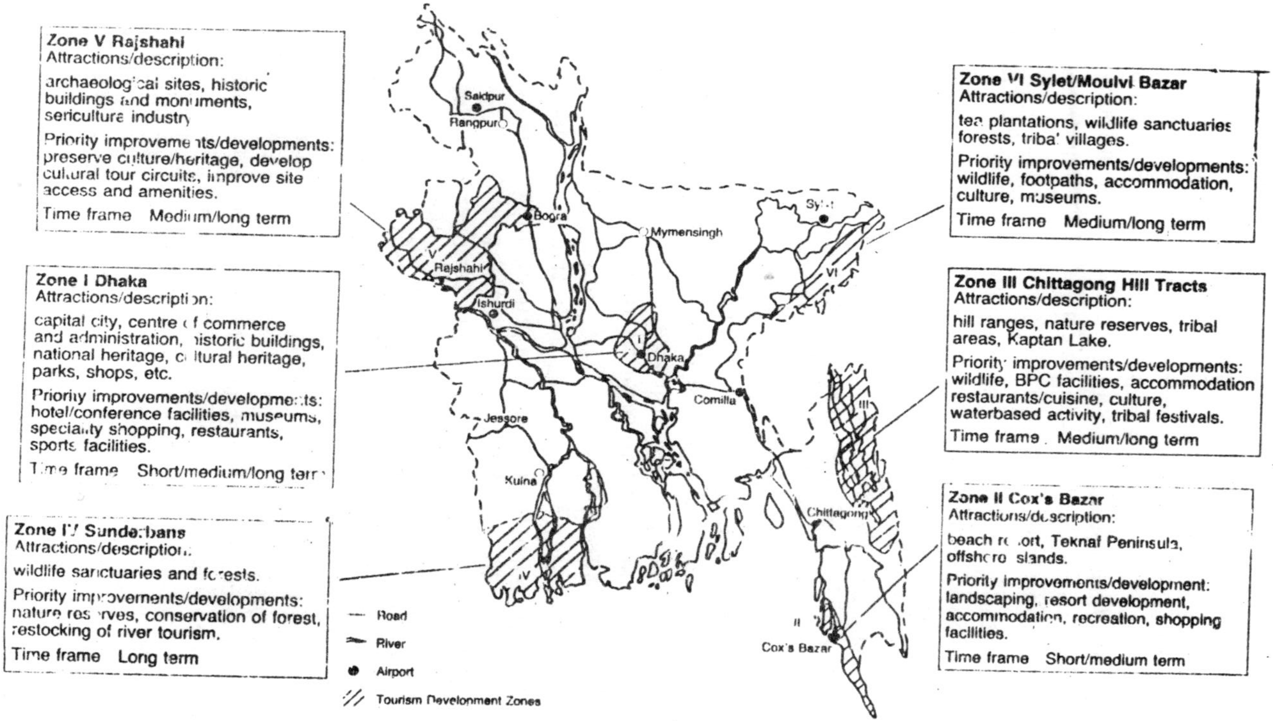

Fig. 8.1 : Bangladesh tourism development zones.

appropriate for a country with limited existing tourism development and various obstacles to overcome in order to achieve expansion of tourism. The tourist attractions identified take account of both natural and cultural features. Emphasis is appropriately given to capitalising on what is unique about the country, especially the riverine environment and possibilities for village tourism. The importance of conservation of natural and archaeological/historic features in the development of tourism, and how this sector can help achieve conservation objectives, is justifiably emphasised.

An important planning principle is applied in the designation of tourism zones, each focused on its own particular cluster of attraction features. The staging of development in these zones is also recommended. The types of tourism which can be developed, based on the specific features of the country, are logically identified. The types of tourism recommended are also practical ones which can be developed at reasonable costs.

Institutional and regulatory ways to implement development according to the plan are indicated. The tourism development programme includes project profile. It is often desirable to prepare project profiles in order to give the government a sound basis for justifying inclusion of the projects in the overall country development programme.

The marketing strategy is realistic in that it recognises the value of selective marketing, and that product improvements will need to be carried out before substantial promotion can be undertaken. It is also an appropriate strategy in realising that Bangladesh can be marketed as a stopover visit for some tourists who are making a multi-country tour of Asia. Recommending cooperation on marketing efforts with other South Asian countries is a sound approach. The marketing strategy could also include the need to portray a favourable but realising image of the country. Image building is especially important in Bangladesh because of the international publicity that has taken place about the natural disasters which periodically occur in the country.

9

Tourism Development in Cyprus

The tourism development strategy for the Republic of Cyprus reflects the approach of aiming for sustainable development of an already substantially developed tourist destination, while still expanding tourism as a major economic sector of the country.

Background

Cyprus is situated in the eastern Mediterranean Sea south of Turkey. The population of the Republic is close to 600,000. It has an extensive coastline with numerous beaches and coastal plains. Much of the southern interior is occupied by the scenic, forested Troodos Mountains. These are flanked by the central plain, where the capital city of Nicosia is located, and the coastal lowlands.

The country has a long history of prehistoric development, followed by successive periods of Classical and Hellenistic Greek, Roman, Byzantine, Frankish, Turkish and British occupation, and now independence. This history has left a rich heritage of archaeological and historic sites, picturesque villages and cultural traditions. The mild climate of Cyprus is one of the major general attractions for tourists.

Tourism in Cyprus in the twentieth century has undergone several changes. Before independence in 1960, tourism was small scale, based on the cool mountain environment. During the early post-independence years, there was greater emphasis on coastal tourism, appealing to a wider international market. Since partition of the island in 1974, coastal tourism has experienced dramatic growth, making the country a mass tourist destination by the early 1980s. By then, concern was being expressed about the future direction of tourism, and the emphasis was shifted somewhat away from quantitative to more qualitative development.

Expansion of tourism has been considerable since the early 1980s, with tourist arrivals reaching almost 1 million in 1987 and 1.7 million in 1990. The great majority of tourists are from Western Europe, with much smaller numbers from the Middle East and North America. Domestic tourism, mostly day trips, is also substantial in the country.

By the mid-1980s, there was still concern about the direction that tourism was taking. Environmental degradation was commencing in the more developed tourism areas, and coastal tourism, focused on the beaches, was by far the dominant form.

Most tourism development had taken place in five main coastal regions. The typical from of development was that the higher class multi-storeyed hotels occupied prime sites adjacent to the best beaches. Lower category accommodation of smaller hotels and hotel apartments were situated on the less desirable sites, often with poor access and views to the beaches. There was very limited tourism in the mountains despite their scenic beauty, interesting historic villages and cool temperatures. The central plain area attracted few holiday tourists, although conference tourism is being developed in Nicosia. Often visited by tourists, the archaeological and historic sites were not primary attractions, and were not always well interpreted to tourists.

Tourism Planning Approach

The continued concern about tourism led to preparation of a comprehensive tourism development plan for the country in the late 1980s (UNDP and WTO, 1988. *Comprehensive Tourism Development Plan for Cyprus*. Madrid: WTO). The planning approach takes into account economic, social and environmental considerations. First, the macro-economic aims of the government up to the year 2001 are analysed, and the economic growth implications are translated into development requirements. Market analyses for international and domestic tourism are made and the product changes needed are assessed.

An important element of the planning approach is an environmental and planning analysis. This includes carrying capacity studies. An appraisal of existing development was carried out of each of the tourism areas, including assessment of the infrastructure. Based on these background analyses, the major development opportunities and constraints are identified. The tourism development strategy is formulated, first as alternative options, and then finalised. Implementation techniques are specified. Environmental improvement plans are presented for certain priority tourism areas in order to demonstrate the local planning approach that could be applied.

The three major objectives of tourism are specified based on present government policies, as follows:

- Growth of tourism's contribution to the Gross Domestic Product (GDP).
- Protection of the environmental and cultural qualities of Cyprus.
- Attraction of higher expenditure tourists.

The potential conflict between the first two objectives is recognised in the plan—that growth might take place at the expense of the environment and culture. This is envisaged to be somewhat reconciled by the third objective of higher spending tourists. Also, the plan's recommendations on improving and controlling development will result in environmental and cultural quality improvements and protection.

The market growth targets are prepared for five-year periods up to 2001. These targets are quantified and expressed in five different ways—contribution of tourism to the GDP; gross expenditures of tourists; number of tourist arrivals; number of total bed-nights; and number of additional tourist beds required. The emphasis of market mix is on attracting higher spending tourists. This implies improving and diversifying the tourism product.

The environmental and planning analysis is approached primarily from the tourist viewpoint—what tourists expect in terms of an interesting, attractive, non-polluted and non-congested environment, and how the environmental quality of Cyprus compares to that of competing destinations. In analysing the environment, the tourism areas were divided into two distinct categories—the coastal areas and the mountain hinterlands. The mountain area is examined generally and the coastal urban tourism areas are analysed in detail, noting the development opportunities and problems. Overall social impact is also evaluated with existing and potential problems identified.

In the environmental analysis, the plan indicates that the beaches form an essential element of the tourism product. Therefore, the quality and capacity of beaches are analysed in detail. The quality analysis is related to whether the beach is sand or shingle, its accessibility and the safety of the adjacent water for bathing. In assessing capacity, the area of beach suitable for tourist use was surveyed, and the beach length and width recorded. Different standards were adopted for different beach qualities, and high and low capacity estimates made. The high and low capacity estimates provide guidelines which show the differences between intensive and non-intensive use of the beach. For example, for sand beaches, the plan uses the standard of 8 square metres per person using the beach as the high estimate, and 12 square metres per person as the low estimate. The beach carrying capacities are calculated for each beach area and for the entire country.

The plan summarises the major development problems and opportunities. The most significant problem is identified as the threat of environmental degradation in most existing coastal tourism areas. The major opportunities are seen as being the resource capacity to further expand coastal tourism and to expand the tourism product and development areas. More tourism development can be undertaken in the mountain region, including the traditional villages there, and presentation of archaeological and historic sites can be improved.

Tourism Development Strategy

Various alternative development strategies are considered in the plan, of which two basic options are presented:

- Continuation of present trends, which represent a *laissez-faire* approach toward development and limited government intervention.
- Controlled growth, which would involve a greater degree of government control on location, quantity and the types of development.

The controlled growth strategy is adopted as the best approach. This strategy implies that much stronger links be forged between the public and private sectors. It aims at providing a sound basis for participants in tourism development to work jointly in achieving balanced and coordinated growth. The plan indicates that the controlled growth strategy defines the amount of development that should take place to meet targets, and makes proposals on its type and location within the context of market and physical planning criteria.

Within the framework of the controlled growth strategy, the plan states that there are two distinct ways in which regional development strategies can be formulated—from the physical planning and environmental viewpoints. One is to open up new tourism areas where new types of development take place to meet the requirements of an up-market improved product. The second way is to consolidate development within the existing tourism areas, where new types of development can be used to intensify the built environment, to give it more form, structure and identity than at present. The development strategy of consolidation is recommended for the following reasons :

- Existing under utilised infrastructure would be more efficiently used.
- Opportunities would be created to give definition, form and identity to specific areas instead of an anonymous 'could be anywhere' image.
- The tourism areas would provide a better range of accommodation and facilities and be more attractive to tourists than at present.
- Revenues to the district and improvement boards would be increased from the intensified development.
- Improvements could be undertaken because more funds would be available for the more developed areas.

The plan emphasises that the strategy of consolidation would make an important contribution to the much needed environmental improvements necessary to upgrade the product. A strategy of dispersal would appeal to land speculators and developers, and leave most of the existing tourism areas in their present environmentally poor condition. Based on this controlled strategy of consolidation, the projected number of tourist beds needed to meet the market targets are distributed among the existing tourism areas. This allocation is made according to the results of the environmental and planning analysis. The plan states that a much greater diversity in the range of facilities and activities offered to tourists will be required to attract higher spending, as well as more tourists during the lower season. Some possible new facilities and activities are suggested. Also to reduce seasonality, new types of market segments are identified. These include retired persons, winter sun market, conference tourists, incentive markets and special interest groups.

In the development programme, recommendations are made on several factors—the quantity, location and type of development, investment incentives; tourism institutional structures; development controls; need for preparation of detailed tourism development plans and beach improvement schemes; environmental issues; product improvements needed; improving the presentation of archaeological and historic sites; and village upgrading schemes. Recommendations are made on tourism employment and training needs. A marketing strategy and promotion programme are recommended. The plan emphasises that successful implementation of the controlled development strategy will depend on controlling the quantity, type and location of development, effective institutional structures, and the incentives offered for development of new tourism products.

Conclusions

The Cyprus plan is an interesting example of formulating future development strategies for sustainable tourism in an already substantially developed and successful tourist destination, but one that is overly dependent on a single type of tourism and commencing to suffer from environmental problems in the tourism areas. These strategies are established within the framework of the government's objectives to continue expanding tourism for its economic benefits and, at the same time, improve environmental and cultural quality.

The planning approach is a comprehensive one which examines all the major aspects of tourism. An important element of the approach is the environmental and planning analysis, including carrying capacity analysis, of the existing and potential tourism areas. It is important to understand present environmental problems as a basis for recommending how to improve the areas. It additionally provides the environmental parameters for recommending the type and extent of suitable future development.

As is the case in many beach resort areas, the capacity of the beaches in Cyprus is the critical factor in establishing carrying capacities. Infrastructure is also examined with respect to carrying capacities of tourism areas. Although the environmental analysis is focused on maintaining tourist satisfaction levels, consideration is also given to the social impact of tourism on residents.

Based on evaluating alternative options, the plan rationally recommends the controlled growth development strategy as the best one to achieve the development objectives. Within that framework, the plan recommends controlled growth at the regional levels through consolidation of the present tourism areas as being the best way to improve the environmental quality of these areas. Controlled growth is a general concept and not necessarily easy to accomplish. The plan provides specific guidelines by specifying the number of tourist beds that should be allowed within each of the tourism areas.

The plan emphasises that implementation of the strategy will require more government intervention. It rightfully points out that application of development controls will be particularly important to implement controlled growth. Investment incentives will be needed to encourage development of new products. In addition to proposing future strategies, the plan recognises that improvements need to be made in existing tourism areas. It makes recommendations on the types of improvements that are required.

The plan justifiably takes account of the opportunity to diversify the tourism product based on the tourism resources of the country. This diversification can expand the tourist markets and reduce the seasonality factor. Through both product improvements and marketing strategies, the objectives of attracting higher spending tourists can be achieved.

10

Tourism Development in Mongolia

The tourism development strategy for Mongolia is related closely to the particular natural and cultural attractions of the country. It aims at giving tourists direct exposure to traditional Mongolian life styles and the distinctive environment of the country.

Background

Mongolia is located in central Asia, bordered on the south, east and west by China and on the north by the Federal Republic of Russia. The country is large, extending almost 2,400 kilometres east and west. The western half of the country is very mountainous, with much of this region having elevations above 2,000 metres and some mountains rising above 3,000 metres. Dense forests and grasslands cover large areas of this region. A great variety of wildlife, including elk, various species of deer and gazelles, bear, sable, wolf, boar, fox and the rare Argall sheep and snow leopard live in the mountains.

Across the eastern part of the country stretches the vast grasslands of the Asian steppe. The steppe grades into the Gobi Desert, which extends through southern Mongolia and into northern China. The Gobi is mostly gravelly, but also contains large areas of sand dunes in the drier portion of the desert near the southern border. The country experiences long, cold winters, but most days throughout the year are clear and sunny.

Although large in size, Mongolia has a small population of about 2.2 million. About a quarter of the people live in the capital city of Ulan Bator. Other cities and towns including provincial capitals are widely dispersed throughout the country. Nomadic herdsmen live on the steppes. Traditionally, Mongolians are Buddhist. Agriculture, mostly animal husbandry, is the basic sector of the economy. Industry is expanding rapidly and is based on processing of agricultural products and mining of coal and minerals. The economic system of Mongolia is currently undergoing change from socialist to free market.

The attractions for tourists in Mongolia are the wide variety of landscapes and wildlife, historic feature including monasteries, temples and palaces, and the living traditions of the nomadic way of life. Although now in ruins, an important archaeological site is Karakorum, capital of the Genghis Khan empire. More generally, the mystique associated with Mongolia's large-scale landscapes, interesting history and nomadic way of life is appealing to tourists.

In the late 1980s, some 10,000 holiday tourists were visiting Mongolia annually. Somewhat over a half of these were from the Western countries and Japan. A relatively small but economically important type of tourists are hunters who pay very high prices for hunting arrangements and permits. The remainder of tourists were mostly from the former USSR and Eastern European countries. Most tourists came on group tours. In addition to the holiday tourists, there is official travel by delegations from other countries.

Access to the country is by air to the international airport at Ulan Bator and by rail connections to Moscow and Beijing. Although roads are being improved, most long-distance travel within the country is by domestic air flights. In 1988, there were about 1,200 tourist beds available—in two hotels in Ulan Bator and three tourist camps, including a camp in the Gobi Desert.

Tourism Planning Approach

The national tourism plan for Mangolia was prepared in 1989 (UNDP and WTO. 1989. *National Tourism Plan for Mongolia.* Madrid. WTO), The plan examines all aspects of tourism. It recommends a development strategy for 2005, implementation policies, development programme for 1990 to 1995, and plans for demonstration projects. The objectives of the planning study are stated in the plan, as follows :

- Identify a concept for tourism which reflects the particular characteristics of Mongolia in relation to international market opportunities.
- Increase the scale of international tourism with a view to earning more foreign currency.
- Develop tourist centres in parts of the country with different characteristics to widen visitors' choice and to assist in the dispersal of economic activity.
- Devise forms of tourism development which are most cost effective in terms of the level of investment required in relation to the length of the season, and to minimise foreign exchange leakage.
- Improve existing services and facilities for tourists, and establish future standards appropriate to the identified markets.
- Provide opportunities for the diversification and restructuring of the economy and for the creation of cooperatives and small business enterprises.
- Miminise in the process any adverse social, cultural or environmental impacts.

Basic studies are presented first in the plan—geographic analysis; review of the overall economy; examination of all types of transportation; description of the present status of tourism; survey and evaluation of tourist attractions; evaluation of the institutional framework; and planning parameters and guidelines. Tourist attractions are categorised into scenic and natural, historic, architectural and archaeological. The planning parameters identify constraints, opportunities and special problems.

The development strategy is divided into the development concept, development of market targets, communication (transportation) and socio-economic implications. Several types of implementation policies are recommended—institutional structures; marketing and promotion strategy; improvement in services; collection and analysis of tourism statistics; and import substitution and new supply industry opportunities. The development programme is divided into the promotion programme and programme of projects and policy implementation. The demonstration projects include two tourist camps and visitor facilities at a major historic monument.

The market analysis considers general world tourist market trends and analyses several specific national markets. The views of the international travel trade are taken into account. Problems seen by the travel trade are the lack of information about tourism in Mongolia and a weak image of the country as a destination. The plan concludes that future tourism growth must be supply led. The overall tourism product needs improving, expanding and diversifying before much further growth can take place. Also there is a problem of extreme seasonality, with half of the holiday tourist arrivals occurring during July and August.

The plan identifies Western Europe, North America and Japan as the major source markets for Mongolia. Market targets, based on achieving an optimum supply/demand balance, were established by year from 1990 to 1995 and for 2000 and 2005. The 2005 target figure is about four times the present number of arrivals. This represents an annual growth rate of 8 per cent. Accommodation bed needs are projected based on the market targets.

Tourism Development Strategy

The tourism development strategy is illustrated in Figure 10.1. The plan explains the key elements of the development strategy. It states that the central feature which makes Mongolia special to tourists is the quality of the rural environment, coupled with the traditional life style of its inhabitants. The image that should be promoted is multi-faceted—the range of different landscapes; the richness of flora and fauna; places of exceptional scenic interest; the absence of development except in traditional nomadic camps; and the overall sense of isolation and tranquillity. To experience this ambience of Mongolia, tourists should be able to visit different parts of the country and pursue their general and special interests. Therefore, product development should focus on devising tourist circuits and excursions. Accommodation should duplicate the traditional rural forms to the extent possible, and be located in scenic areas. However, recreation and leisure facilities will still need to be provided for tourists.

The plan recommends that most of the tourist accommodation (outside of Ulan Bator) be in the form of camps in rural areas, so that tourists can experience the natural landscapes and traditional

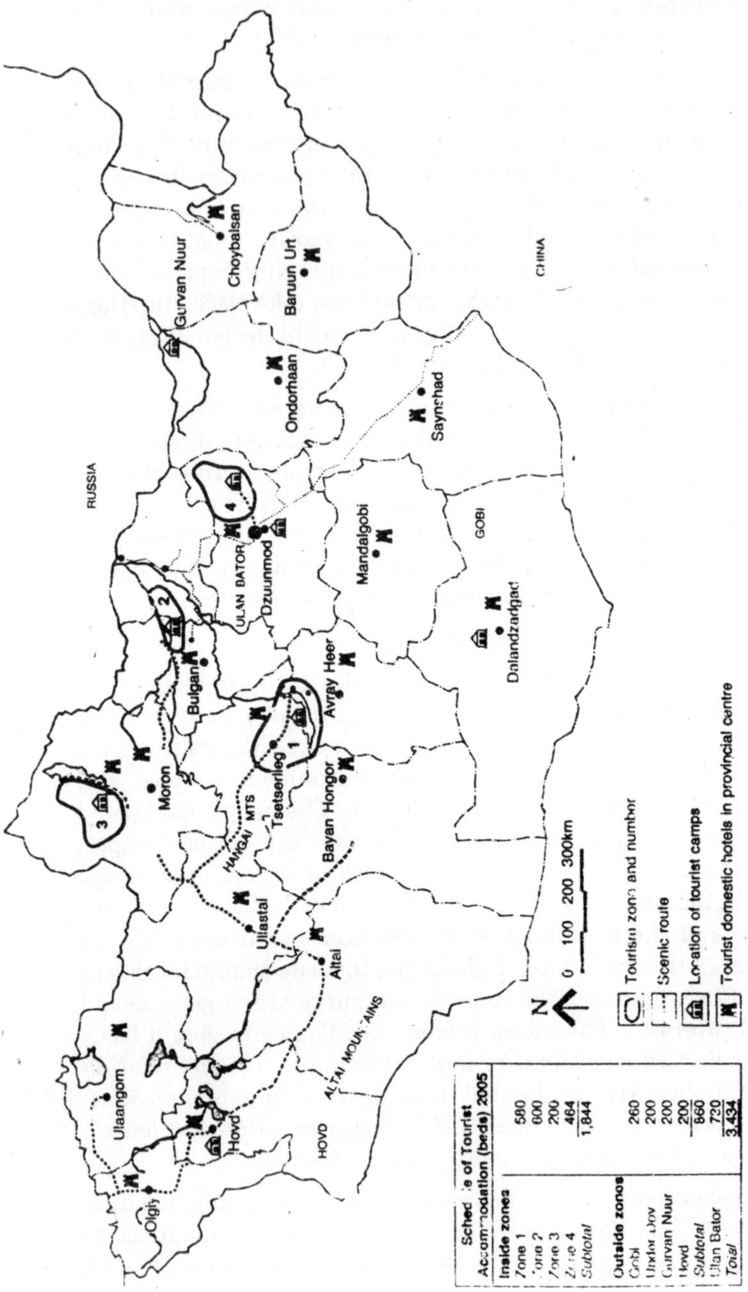

Fig. 10.1 : Mongolia tourism development strategy map.

way of life. The plan points out that, in addition to the preference of tourists, expansion of existing and development of new camps offer several advantages, as follows :

- Formed as they of *gers* (traditional tented homes), the camps are somewhat characteristic of the nomadic life style and are ideally suited to the rural environment, being low profile and unobtrusive.
- The sleeping component is the *ger*, which is inexpensive and portable, and components requiring use of permanent materials are limited. This reduces the capital cost to a level which can be recovered from the revenue earned over the short summer season.
- The *gers* are made in Mongolia, mainly of locally available materials, with only sanitary and utility fittings and equipment required to be imported.
- The camps can be constructed relatively rapidly and are easy to expand.

The plan states that camps should be located in the countryside in those areas that have particularly interesting or typical landscapes, and where there are opportunities to observe wildlife. The proximity to some special natural or historical features would be an advantage. Reasonably good access to an airfield is important, but this should not intrude into the camp surroundings. To prevent a sense of overcrowding, the plan emphasises that the camps should be restricted in size to about 200 beds, except in special circumstances. The camps should be designed to offer a mix of two, three and four beds per *ger*, with 75 *gers* generally being the maximum number allowed in each camp. The maximum development density should be 25 *gers* per hectare, plus any land needed for outdoor recreational facilities.

Sanitary facilities should be provided to a minimum standard of one sanitary unit for every 10 beds. These units would be grouped into two to four blocks distributed around the camp. Each camp would have a restaurant (preferably in a large *ger*), a bar, administrative offices, stores and indoor leisure facilities, as well as a range of outdoor recreational facilities. The plan sets forth standards for sanitary and solid waste disposal, electric power supply and water heating. Solar power is recommended to be used when it is feasible to develop.

The strategy identifies various tourism zones throughout the country, within which most of the tourist facilities should be located. These zones are selected based on certain location criteria, as follows :

- Combination of high environmental quality and a relative concentration of historical/architectural features.
- Exceptional environmental quality.
- Distinctive landscape forms and a variety of wildlife habitats.
- Availability of several locations suitable for the development of tourist camps.
- Capacity to absorb a number of facilities.

Consideration is also given to the location of existing facilities or firm proposals for new ones.

Four inner tourism zones are designated relatively near to Ulan Bator in the north central part of the country, and four outer zones are recommended in more remote places including the Gobi Desert and western mountains. The projected accommodation beds are distributed among these zones. Some new beds are allocated for expansion of existing camps. A total of some 13 camps (six existing and seven proposed) are envisaged. Some accommodation is also allocated to Ulan Bator. The plan states that small hotels for use by holiday tourists and local business travellers could be developed in the provincial capitals.

An important part of the development strategy is to make Mongolia more attractive to tourists in those aspects where it has special advantages. To achieve this, various types of activities are recommended to be developed—horse riding, pony trekking, wildlife observation and fishing. Facilities and services would be developed in the camps for tourists to engage in those activities. Special interest tours and hunting are also identified as having potential. The plan examines excursion itineraries that can be made from the camps. Because of the limited extent of improved road network and substantial travel distances, it is difficult and not always interesting for tourists to undertake long excursions. However, excursions can be organised to visit local features near to the camps—horse and camel farms; nomadic encampments;

some outstanding monasteries; archaeological sites; and areas of scenic and environmental interest.

The plan makes recommendations for transportation, noting that air access to and within the country is already good, as is the rail access. However, the present condition of the road network and the distances involved do not make long-distance land travel by tourists feasible. Therefore, the strategy is designed so as not to rely on extensive road travel. The domestic air service will remain the primary means for tourists to visit various parts of the country and reach the camps.

The marketing strategy emphasises that marketing efforts should be directed to enhancing the appeal of Mongolia across a broader spectrum of tourist types, both general and special interest tourists. Priority should be given to image-creation of the country as a destination. During the short–term, it is envisaged that group tours will continue to be the appropriate market to target. Over the longer-term, more independent tourists can be attracted, as tourist facilities and infrastructure are improved. During the short-term, the existing major markets of North America, Western Europe and Japan should receive the main thrust of promotional efforts. Over the longer-term, more attention can be given to emerging markets in Asia.

Conclusions

The tourism development strategy for Mongolia logically focuses on the unique features of the country and how these can best be experienced by tourists. Other important considerations are to minimise the investment capital required for development, and to provide opportunities for cooperatives and small business enterprises. The approach of developing traditional tented camps is an imaginative one that will allow tourists to experience life in rural Mongolia. Such camps are relatively inexpensive to develop and Mongolians already have some experience in their operation. Using the camps as a base, activities can be organised for tourists. These will give them some exposure to nomadic life styles, horse riding for which Mongolia is well known, scenic places, wildlife and important archaeological and historic sites.

The plan applies the basic planning principle of designating tourism zones, with Ulan Bator being maintained as the gateway and staging area for the country. Ulan Bator has hotels, museums, theatre performances and other attraction features which can induce tourists to stay there for one or two days on their entry to and departure from the country. The zones are located based on application of realistic criteria, including accessibility utilising the existing airport network. The more specific location criteria set forth for the tourist camps will provide a valuable guide for the government to use in selecting new camp sites in the future. The standards recommended for planning the camps are ones which will help maintain the tourist sense of isolation and contact with the environment. At the same time, the plan recommends appropriate utility standards so that the camps do not generate any serious environmental problems.

It should be noted that Mongolia has a progressive nature conservation programme. This will reinforce the nature-oriented concept of the tourism development strategy. Several important environmental areas have already been established as national parks and nature reserves, and more parks and reserves have been proposed. Although hunting is allowed and is an important source of tourist income, it is very carefully controlled. The number of permits sold each year for the taking of individual animals is based on maintaining a sustainable population level of those animals. A census of animals is carried out annually as a basis for deciding how many permits to issue in that year. Conservation is also being applied to historic monuments, in some cases with international assistance.

The marketing strategy is realistic. It emphasises the importance of initially developing a definite image of Mongolia as a tourist destination, and the need to broaden the types of tourist markets. It recognises, however, that because of presently limited product development, promotional efforts should first be directed to group tours. When the product is improved in the future, including better tourist services and road infrastructure, promotion can be directed more to individual tourists.

Implementation of this strategy will provide a firm foundation for developing sustainable tourism, at minimal cost, in Mongolia. When this planning period is completed, then further development of tourism can take place based on circumstances prevailing at that time.

11

Tourism Development in Uganda

The tourism development strategy of Uganda applies sound planning principles in establishing a foundation for revitalising the tourism sector in a country that has limited existing facilities, but much-longterm potential.

Background

Uganda is located in east-central Africa, inland from Kenya, east of Zaire and north of Tanzania and Rwanda. The population of the country is somewhat over 17 million, and includes several cultural groups. The capital city of Kampala has about half a million inhabitants. The country contains the northern part of Lake Victoria, the source of the Nile, Murchison Falls, the high snow-capped Ruwenzori Mountains (the Mountains of the Moon) and mountain gorilla reserves.

The primary attractions for tourists are outstanding scenic areas, including lakes, rivers, mountains, rainforests and savanna, and a variety of wildlife. Uganda generally has wetter, more upland and more forested landscapes than do other eastern and southern African countries. This environment offers numerous opportunities for boating, trekking and wildlife viewing. The upland climate is very pleasant for tourists. Ten national parks have been designated although most of these still have limited tourist facilities. Some historic places and traditional cultural patterns comprise interesting secondary attractions.

Tourism was relatively well developed in Uganda in the late 1960s and early 1970s, when it made a significant contribution to the country's economy. Then, because of changes in government policy and political turmoil during the 1970s and early tc mid-1980s, tourism became virtually non-existent. Much of the tourist facility development was seriously damaged or deteriorated from lack of maintenance, as was the country's infrastructure. Much of the wildlife was killed. Commencing in the late 1980s and continuing to the present, rehabilitation of the economy and infrastructure, including revitalisation of tourism, is taking place. Programmes for conservation of wildlife are being vigorously pursued. The animal populations are now expanding, although some species are not yet up to their previous levels.

By the early 1990s, some hotels of international standard were available in Kampala, Entebbe and Queen Elizabeth National Park, but not yet elsewhere in the country. However, there are limited facilities for business travellers and the more adventurous tourists in the towns and in or near most of the national parks. Plans are underway for continued rehabilitation of accommodation and development of new hotels and lodges. Roads are being improved and the parks are becoming more accessible to tourists. The international airport at Entebbe is also being upgraded. Several tour and travel agencies and some other tourist facilities are now in operation.

In 1991, Uganda received 68,000 international tourist arrivals. Only about 10,000 of these were holiday tourists, and the remainder were travellers on business and official missions. Many of the holiday tourists are of the budget type, including 'backpackers' and 'truckers'—tourists travelling overland by truck or van through several countries in Africa. The large international aid community in the country provides many of the present visitors to the national parks.

Recognising the potential importance of tourism as a source of economic development, the government has adopted a policy for developing tourism. Alongwith tourism, the government has some major national park programmes underway, including developing visitor facilities in the parks.

Tourism Planning Approach

A comprehensive tourism planning project for Uganda was carried out in the early 1990s. This included preparation of a national tourism plan (UNDP and WTO, 1993. *Integrated*

Tourism Master Plan—Republic of Uganda, Vols. 1, 2 and 3. Madrid: WTO) and training of government staff in tourism management. A separate project is also underway on establishing a tourism training school for training Ugandans in hotel, catering and tour and travel operations.

The tourism plan is composed of several elements. Various background studies were conducted—an overview of the economy and economic policies; review of tourism-related projects and studies, of which there were many; survey and evaluation of tourist attractions, accommodation and other tourist facilities and services; market prospects; analysis of financial and manpower resources; and the institutional system. Planning parameters and guidelines are established, including identifying the development opportunities and constraints.

The general objective of developing tourism is stated in the plan as follows :

> To develop the tourism sector of the economy to the maximum extent possible, consistent with the protection of environmental and cultural values, as a means for generating wealth, foreign exchange earnings, employment, a public awareness of the international community, and that community's understanding of the attributes of Uganda.

This general objective was further elaborated and specified in the plan.

Based on the background studies and objectives, the national tourism structure plan was prepared. The horizon year of the plan is 2002, with an intermediate period for 1997. Part One of the structure plan deals with the spatial and development strategy—general policy and planning principles; development concept; market development; tourist accommodation and facilities; transport; economic impact analysis; and environmental and social impacts. Part Two of the structure plan comprises planning and development policies—management of tourism planning and development; development of a tourism data base; manpower analysis and training; managing the environment; and implementing the plan.

Plan implementation is given emphasis. The implementation section includes several elements—selection of priority areas; detailed planning for Queen Elizabeth National Park; a development programme for 1993–97; a policy action programme;

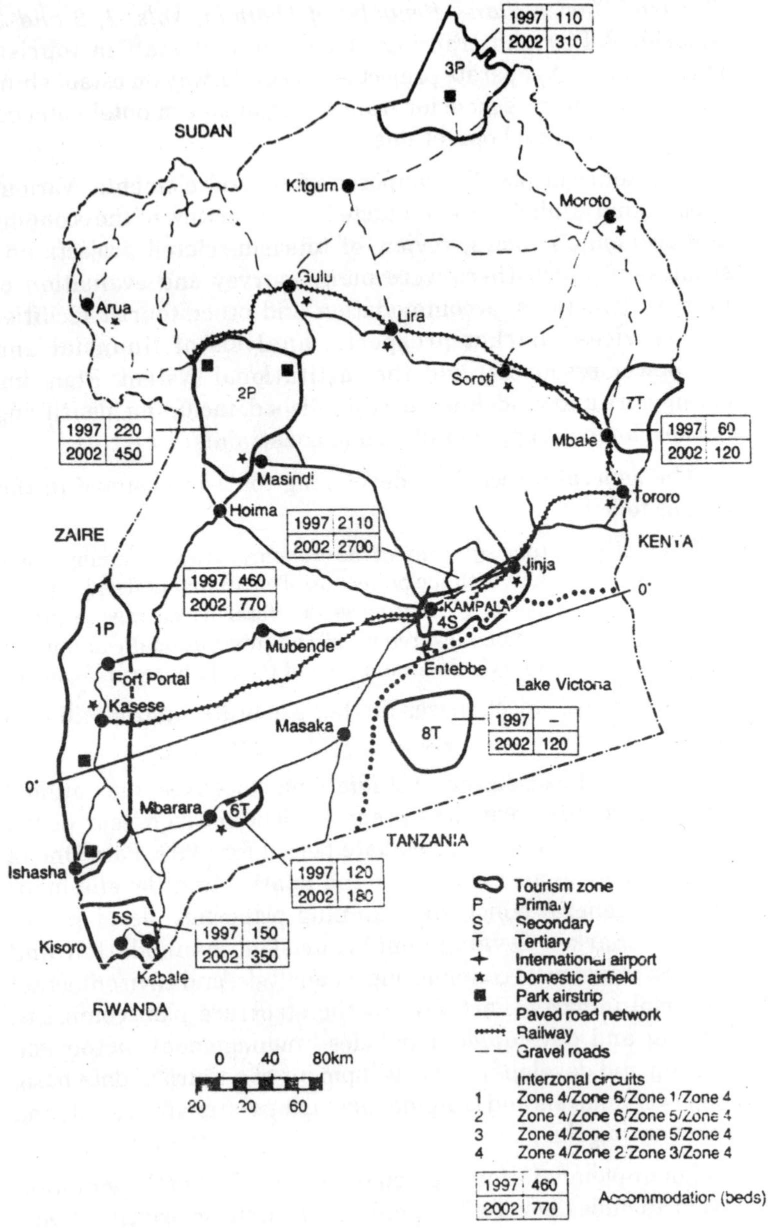

Fig. 11.1 : Uganda tourism development concept.

an implementation manual; and pre-feasibility analyses for several priority projects.

Tourism Development Strategy

The development concept is based on phased development of attractions and related activities as a tourism product of high quality and diversity. The plan states that, during the short and medium-term, game viewing, whilst being the prime attraction, will be an inferior experience to that available elsewhere because the game populations are still being rejuvenated. Game viewing should, however, be combined with other attractions—the general scenic beauty of the country and specific natural features such as Murchison Falls and the river trips on the Nile to reach the falls. Also very important is the adventure tourism potential of the Ruwenzori Mountains, which are excellent for trekking and of much botanical interest. Similarly, the rainforests offer opportunities for different forms of ecotourism, including controlled viewing of primates—mountain gorillas and chimpanzees.

Therefore, the strategy is to create a multi-faceted tourism product while game populations are recovering. This diverse product will provide a special image for Uganda's tourism, which can be further strengthened when the game have reached their former levels.

The plan establishes tourism zones. These are depicted in Figure 11.1 and described as follows :

- *Three primary zones*—The Rift Valley Zone, which includes Queen Elizabeth and Ruwenzori Mountains National Parks and other national parks and game reserves; the Murchison Falls Zone, which includes Murchison Falls National Park and forest and game reserves; and the Kidepo Valley Zone, which includes Kidepo Valley National Park, a forest reserve and controlled hunting areas.
- *Two secondary zones*—The Capital Area Zone which includes Entebbe as the entry point of tourists, Kampala as the country's staging area and focus of business travel, and other points of interest such as the source of the Nile; and the Southwest Mountains Zone which includes two gorilla-based national parks and some outstanding scenic areas of mountains, lakes and forests.

- *Three tertiary zones*—Lake Mburo Zone, which is focused on Lake Mburo National Park; Mount Elgon Zone, which contains Mount Elgon National Park, a major waterfall and scenic beauty; and the Ssese Islands Zone, which includes a group of islands in Lake Victoria known for their scenic beauty and birdlife.

The plan sets forth several tourist circuits which link the zones and will assist in prolonging the stay of tourists. Seven inter-zonal circuits, ranging from four days to three weeks, are recommended. Possibilities for intra-zonal circuits are also identified.

Based on the market analysis (described below), the plan projects the type and number of accommodation required—a total of 5,000 beds by 2002. The projected accommodation beds are allocated to each of the development zones for 1997 and 2002. Figure 11.1 shows the allocation of accommodation for each of the tourism zones for 1997 and 2002. Because of its importance as the business and government centre and the staging area for tourists, the Capital Area Zone receives more than half the beds.

There is a further breakdown of accommodation allocation by year from 1993 to 1997. Because of the time required to build accommodation, no new beds are shown for 1993. A crash programme is recommended to provide additional beds by 1994. These would be in the form of safari camps of high standard. The additional accommodation required after 1994 would be composed of renovated and new hotels and safari lodges and camps. The accommodation would all be developed to medium and high-quality standards, depending on their locations. The plan describes the types of safari lodges and camps that should be developed.

The plan recommends provision of other tourist facilities. These would be in the form of tourist service centres located at the national parks and other major destination points. Three levels of tourist centres are proposed, as follows :

- *Principal tourist centres*—providing a comprehensive range of facilities including a reception and information lobby, a nature interpretation centre, a general service outlet for the issuance of park permits and arranging guides, excursions, transport and tours, a medical clinic and emergency evacuation services, public lavatories and retail services such as a cafe, bar and craft shop.

- *Subsidiary tourist centres*—providing a more limited range of functions and smaller in size.
- *Minor tourist centres*—providing only basic facilities of reception and information, small interpretation displays and public lavatories.

The tourist centres that serve the special needs of adventure tourists would be slightly different. These centres would also include porterage services, a grocery shop and equipment and clothing for sale and rental. Emergency evacuation services will be particularly important for these centres.

The plan sets forth a ten-year programme for development of the tourist centres. Six of these are scheduled for 1993–97 and 11 for 1998–2002.

Recommendations are made for transport. The plan notes that the international airport facility at Entebbe will have adequate capacity when the present programme for renovation is completed. International air links, however, will need to be expanded. The domestic airports are not greatly important for tourism. More important is pursuing the programme for upgrading and continuing maintenance of airstrips in various national parks, in order to provide better access for tourists.

The plan indicates that substantial progress is being made on rehabilitation of the road network, and several tourist destinations can now be comfortably reached by road. The plan lists other roads which still require improvements for tourist use.

On market development, the plan states that, during the short-term period, the marketing and attraction of tourists should be carefully approached. The current restricted capacity of facilities in the tourism zones and the limited possibilities for game viewing will not meet many typical tourists' expectations. When these conditions are improved, marketing can be more aggressively pursued. The projection of tourist arrivals is based on the proposed programme of new accommodation being developed in the tourism zones. Simultaneously, the game populations will have increased, based on present conservation programme objectives. Holiday tourist arrivals are projected to reach 33,000 by 1997, and 66,500 by 2002. Also, there will be substantial numbers of business and other types of arrivals.

By region of origin, the main source markets are identified as Western Europe and the USA. The major market countries to be targeted will be the UK, Germany and the USA, with France and Italy as subsidiary targets. The plan specifies the major market segments—single-destination general interest tourists; multi-destination general interest tourists; regional tourists (residents of neighbouring countries); trekkers; truckers; and special interest tourists. The marketing objectives are stated as follows :

- Cooperate closely with all neighbouring countries.
- Develop as wide a spread of market segments as possible.
- Encourage a wide seasonal spread of tourist arrivals by attracting shoulder and off-peak traffic.
- Attract, where possible, market segments which offer a longer length of stay to obtain an optimum return on marketing costs.
- Direct, where possible, marketing resources to segments that tend to have higher spending patterns.

A subsequent case study examines the promotion strategy and programme for Uganda, based on these market projections and marketing objectives.

The plan reviews environmental impact with respect to several considerations—types of impacts; biological carrying capacity; tourist carrying capacity; and visual and physical impacts. No serious environmental problems are foreseen if the recommendations of this plan and other programmes are followed. However, some types of tourist use must be highly controlled. For example, the viewing of gorillas and chimpanzees must observe strict carrying capacities. For gorilla viewing, visitors should be limited to a party of no more than six over the age of 15, for a period of no more than one hour a day, for any habituated group of gorillas. This control is necessary to avoid unduly disturbing the habits of family groups and to protect the animals from the transmission of potentially fatal human diseases.

Social impact is briefly examined in the plan. No serious social problems are anticipated. However, it is recommended that there be information given to tourists, and that the local population be educated about tourism. This public education will be especially important to make local communities aware of the need to conserve important natural areas from being misused. The plan states that part of this exercise should consist of involving these communities in the introduction of control measures, in the planning of development proposals and in encouraging their participation in the benefits of tourism development.

Conclusions

The Uganda plan examines all aspects of tourism as an integrated system. On the growth of tourism, the plan is justifiably cautious. It recognises that market projections must take into consideration the need to improve and expand the tourism product of facilities, services, attractions and infrastructure. If tourist expectations are raised to an artificially high level and not then met in reality, this can do long-term damage to the image of the country. Therefore, marketing development is kept in harmony with the capabilities of achieving the necessary product improvements.

In formulating the development strategy, the plan applies the fundamental principle of establishing tourism zones based on the attractions available in the zones. This zoning further specifies the different importance levels of the zones. These zones then logically provide the basis for identifying various types and lengths of tourist circuits. The concept of developing tourist service centres—as places where tourism services are consolidated—seems to be an appropriate one that has been successfully used elsewhere. In the project analysis section of the plan, pre-feasibility analyses are conducted for three of the service centres. These analyses will give the government some guidance for development of the centres.

The plan observes that if local communities located near to national parks and conservation areas are involved in tourism, and receive benefits from it, they will more likely be cooperative in supporting the necessary conservation measures. This is an important concept that could be elaborated in the future, and some pilot community projects undertaken.

Implementation of a tourism plan is challenging in a newly developing tourism country. The Uganda plan includes a manual as a specific guide for implementation. This manual is summarised in a subsequent case study.

12

Tourism Development in Philippines

The national tourism development plan for the Philippines is a comprehensive one. It provides short-, medium- and long-term objectives, policies and strategies that aim at correcting current deficiencies while, at the same time, providing the basis for the continued expansion of tourism.

Background

The Republic of the Philippines is situated in Southeast Asia and is a member of the Association of Southeast Asian Nations (ASEAN). It is a relatively large multi-island country with a population of more than 65 million comprising various ethnic groups and religions. The Philippines encompasses a diversity of tourist attractions located throughout the country. These attractions are related to both the natural environment—particularly scenic mountain areas and an extensive coastline offering beaches and marine recreation—and its history and culture.

Tourism is already considerably developed in the country. There were more than 1 million international tourist arrivals in 1990 and some 2 million domestic tourist. About half the foreign tourists come from other countries in East and Southeast Asia, and most of the remainder are from North America and West Europe. The average length of stay of tourists is about 12 days. In 1990, tourism generated approximately US $ 2.5 billion in gross revenues and more than US $ 1 billion in net foreign exchange earnings. Tourism accounted for close to 5 per cent of the Gross Domestic Product and employed an estimated 660,000 persons.

In the 1980s, various problems with respect to tourism development were identified. For the size of the country and its extent of attractions, tourism was still rather small scale. Most of the limited tourism that did exist was concentrated in the National Capital Region of Manila. The growth of tourism had been quite erratic, with rapid reversals in tourist flows, depending on unpredictable events.

Tourism Planning Approach

In order to provide the basis for rectifying existing problems and a logical framework for the expansion of tourism, a tourism development plan was prepared in 1991. (UNDP and WTO, 1991. *Tourism Master Plan for the Republic of the Philippines*. Madrid: WTO). The planning study was organised based on formulating a long-range plan, medium-term development programme, and destination area plans. The long-term horizon year was set for 2010. Planning is based on division of this time frame into a short-term period of 1991–93, medium-term of 1994–96 and long-term of 1997–2010.

The plan uses the integrated approach of examining all the physical, socio-economic and institutional aspects of tourism, with the main report backed up by separate technical reports. Background surveys and analyses were conducted, the major opportunities and constraints for improving and expanding tourism were identified, and objectives, targets, policies and strategies were formulated. The analysis includes a comparative evaluation of ASEAN destinations, and consultations were made in key market areas such as East Asia and Europe. Also important was analysis of transportation access to and within the country. In the review of the current situation of tourism, economic, socio-cultural and environmental impacts were analysed. Alternative strategies were evaluated to arrive at the optimum ones.

A series of workshops were held with the tourism industry and other groups, including the Tourism Committee of the House of Representatives. These workshops focused on identifying the strengths, weaknesses, opportunities and constraints facing tourism, and the strategies that should be applied to develop this sector.

The main conclusions of the background studies on the potential of tourism to expand at a macro level are as follows :

- The tourist markets, and attractions to match these markets, are available and the tourism product can be delivered at a quality standard and price that are competitive in ASEAN.
- The capacity of the economic, social and ecological environment to handle growth is still considerable despite the fact there are certain problems.

However, the physical capacity of the tourism sector is limited by:

- Its ability to move large volumes of tourists to other parts of the Philippines outside the Capital Region.
- The lack of trained human resources at the required standard and quantity.
- Institutional overlap and human resource shortages in the tourism planning, development, financing and management areas.
- Strong competition for public and private sector finance.
- Inappropriate land use planning and development policies that make it difficult to readily develop large resorts.
- Unpredictable events such as earthquakes, volcanic eruptions, regional conflicts, internal political disputes and insurgency.

The plan indicates that these factors limit the total volume of foreign and domestic tourists that the country can expect to host, unless a programme of action is undertaken to remove these constraints to expansion.

Tourism Development Objectives, Strategies and Policies

The long-range objectives of tourism development are designed to balance economic interests with socio-cultural and environmental issues. These objectives are stated as follows:

- Optimise the contribution of tourism to economic growth at the national and regional levels (including spreading the benefits of tourism throughout the country).
- Enhance and contribute to social cohesion and cultural preservation at the local level (including encouraging development that is sensitive to the needs of local people and conservation of cultural heritage).

- Develop tourism on an environmentally sustainable basis (including limiting development to the carrying capacity of the environment and encouraging environmental conservation).
- Develop a diversity of destinations, attractions and markets to minimise exposure to major internal and external threats to tourism activity.

The plan observes that the expansion of tourism will depend greatly on the level of investment that can be made, especially of scarce public sector resources.

After evaluation of alternative development strategies to achieve these objectives, the study recommends a three-point strategy as follows :

- Adopt a cluster development approach based on the establishment of three main international gateways and associated satellite destinations.
- Adopt a niche and mass market approach based on a diverse mix of special interest, vacation, resort, convention, exhibition, touring and incentive travel products.
- Work toward a balance of development between foreign and domestic tourism.

Based on the development objectives and strategies, domestic and foreign tourist market targets are established for the short-, medium- and long-term periods. These are expressed in terms of both tourist arrivals and tourist nights, with domestic tourist targets calculated only for those using commercial accommodation. The targets indicate considerable growth of tourism for 2010—about five times the 1990 figure for foreign tourists and 10 times the 1990 figure for domestic tourists. The main source of foreign markets are targeted from East Asia, with the majority of foreign tourists being resort oriented.

The plan recommends implementation of development strategies for the short-, medium- and long-term periods. Short-term development should be focused on several actions—completing key infrastructure projects; making use of existing tourist attractions, facilities and markets; planning future infrastructure and resort projects; removing policy constraints;

and streamlining the institutional structure. During the medium-term, emphasis should be placed on expanding key infrastructure and developing new resorts according to the development strategy, and establishing tourism training facilities. In the longer-term, the development strategy should be consolidated with continued development of emerging and potential destination areas in each of the clusters.

The cluster development strategy is based on the concept that each cluster is served by one or more international gateways, linked to a variety of satellite destinations. Each satellite would have its own unique theme. Figure 12.1 illustrates this development approach. One cluster is the Luzon- or Manila-based cluster, with Manila as the gateway, and includes several destinations in the northern and eastern parts of the country. Another cluster is the Visayas- or Cebu-based cluster, with Cebu as the gateway, and includes the central Philippines. The third is the Mindanao- or Davao-based cluster, with Davao as the gateway, and includes destinations in the southern part of the country. Short-, medium- and long-term targets of tourist arrivals are established for each of these tourism regions.

The plan recommends implementation policies for various major elements of tourism. Accommodation policies are focused on developing accommodation outside the capital region, especially in the Visayas and Mindanao clusters. Incentives should be offered to upgrade existing and develop new accommodation in these regions. New resorts would be developed in these regions, as well as the northern part of the Luzon region, and infrastructure constructed to serve the resorts. Marketing should be directed to promoting places outside the Manila area.

Transportation policies relate mostly to air transport. The plan recommends that a more flexible approach be adopted to approve charter and scheduled air services, and that additional domestic and international air carriers be allowed to serve secondary airports in the country. Domestic and international terminal facilities at the main gateways should be expanded. Also, domestic air operation should be deregulated and more competition encouraged among domestic carriers. Recommendations are made on road, sea and rail transportation within the country.

The plan recommends that marketing policies be implemented in three phases. During the short-term period, the focus should be on several efforts–raising the present low accommodation occupancies; improving the international tourist image with regard to stability and security; improving the image for tourism investors; and improving service and access to entertainment,

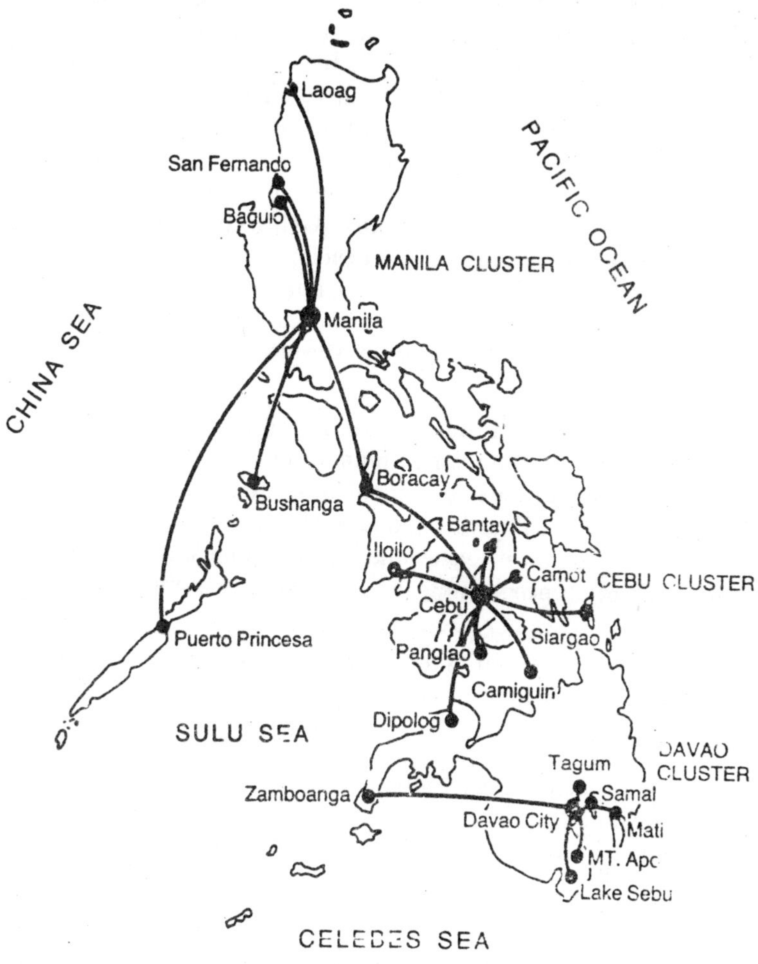

Fig. 12.1 : Tourism cluster development areas and satellite destinations, Philippines.

restaurants, shopping and tours. Over the medium-term, the marketing policy should be to start to project the Philippines as a major and revived tourist destination aiming at a wide spectrum of markets, but particularly at the emerging domestic and East Asian markets. For the long-term, the policy should seek to build upon the initiatives established previously, but diversify the Philippines into a major world destination.

The main thrust of the product development policy should be to upgrade and diversify the existing range of products in various ways. One recommended approach is to focus on properly developing one or two attractions in each of the gateways, including creating at least one major attraction in or near each of these. Another policy is to improve access to and information about existing products, and upgrade the standard of existing tour products and programmes. Other policies are also recommended—encouraging the development of additional day visitor activities at destination areas; improving the reliability of domestic transportation services; and creating new resort, special interest and tour products based on the particular features of the country.

The plan points out that the existing training system will not be able to produce the trained manpower needed in the future. The main thrust of the training policies is to establish a Tourism Industry Training Board, regional training centres in the three tourism regions, an internationally acceptable standard facility and certification programme, and faculty development.

The policies recommended on development standards and guidelines are reviewed in detail in a separate case study in this publication.

Conclusions

The approach to the Philippines plan is a comprehensive and integrated one that is adapted for a country which already has a somewhat established tourism sector, but one that requires stabilisation and appropriate policies to guide its future development. The plan is particularly focused on identifying the present opportunities and constraints of tourism as a basis for recommending objectives, strategies and policies. The planning analysis reveals a problem (and opportunity) that is common to many tourism countries—the need for diversification of the tourism product, especially of tourist attractions and activities, in order to attract a broader base of tourist markets and effectively compete with destinations elsewhere. The plan also makes the important point that tourism should be developed for sustainable use of resources.

The plan identifies another common problem—the concentration of tourism in a single area and the neglect of other tourism areas that have potential for development. As the plan emphasises, this leads to limited distribution of the benefits of tourism, as well as a limited tourism product. The plan also recognises the disruption that natural disasters and political disturbances can have on maintaining consistent tourist arrival patterns.

To overcome these problems and take advantage of opportunities, the plan uses the principle of establishing tourism regions, called clusters in this plan, each of which is focused on a regional gateway. Within the regions are designated development areas or satellite destinations. At the regional level, emphasis is placed on development of integrated resorts, another important planning principle for large-scale tourism. This development strategy provides a rational basis for dispersing development, whilst still containing it in specific places for ease of providing access and infrastructure and other reasons.

The national level market targets are allocated to the various regions. This provides not only a guide for the specific level of development in each region, but also allows for flexibility of development within the regions. The multiple regional gateways allow for flexibility of arrival and departure access points to a relatively large country, also a basic planning principle.

In the implementation of the strategy, the plan applies a very useful approach of recommending policies for each of the key elements of tourism, including institutional factors. This provides the government and private sector with guidelines for actions that need to be taken. For example, the need to improve the international tourism image of the country is an important marketing strategy that is recommended to be undertaken, as well as specific promotional techniques. The plan further sets forth a detailed medium-term development programme and destination area plans as specific guides for decision-making.

In the staging of development implementation, the plan recommends a realistic short-term approach that focuses on making better use of existing facilities. At the same time, it lays the foundation for change through infrastructure planning and development and institutional improvements. Then, over the medium and long-term, there is gradual implementation of the regional cluster concept and controlled dispersal of tourism.

This plan provides the overall basis for rational development of tourism. It will need to be followed by other studies such as for development of special interest and ecotourism, as part of the product enrichment programme.

13

Resort Development in Mexico

The strategy for development of integrated resorts in Mexico represents a national level policy approach adopted for developing beach resorts as a major form of tourism in the country. An important aspect of this strategy is the financial and organisational mechanisms established to implement it.

Background

Situated in North America, Mexico is a relatively large country of some 90 million people. It has extensive coastlines facing onto the Pacific Ocean, Gulf of Mexico and Caribbean Sea. With many beaches and marine areas, scenic landscapes, pleasant climate, major archaeological and historic sites and highly interesting cultural patterns, Mexico offers a full range of attractions for tourists. Its location next to the USA and not far from Canada provides the country with large nearby tourist markets.

Mexico has a long tradition of domestic tourism with beach resorts having been particularly popular with Mexicans. International tourism, based mostly on the American market, commenced substantial development after World War II. The west coast beach resort of Acapulco became especially popular with both domestic and foreign tourists. Also, tourists were, and still are, attracted to the major cities and archaeological sites. There was, and still is, considerable 'border' tourism developed near the boundary with the USA. However, by the 1960s, it became clear to the government that tourism in the country was lagging behind Hawaii, the Caribbean and other destinations.

In examining the country's potential for development, the government identified tourism as a sector that could generate substantial employment, income and foreign exchange earnings. A detailed analysis of tourism was carried out by the Bank of Mexico during 1966–68. This revealed that tourism was developing rapidly internationally, with much potential for continued growth, but that Mexico was not adequately participating in tourism. The study identified several problems—the country had no long-term tourism policy; no tourism programme existed that established concrete objectives; there were no functioning financial instruments for development and promotion; and no criteria had been adopted for planning and development. Tourist facilities were excessively concentrated in Acapulco. Some newer resort areas had occurred spontaneously and possessed obvious weaknesses. This situation led to adoption of a resort development policy and strategy.

Since the late 1960s, tourism has grown considerably in Mexico. By 1990, there were more than 6 million foreign tourist arrivals, plus a much larger number of excursionists who visited the border zone for short stays. Most foreign tourists are Americans and Canadians, with a limited number from Europe. The average length of stay of foreign tourists is slightly more than 10 days. International tourism receipts contribute more than US $ 5 billion to the national economy. Domestic tourism also has remained an important tourist market.

Resort Development Strategy

Following on from the study of the late 1960s, diversification of tourism was considered to be the priority approach. (This description of the development strategy is taken from the publication *Tourist Resorts—a Mexican Strategy for Development*, published by FONATUR in 1988 in Mexico City.) Within that framework, the policy was decided to be that of upgrading existing resorts and developing new ones. The new resorts would be developed based on the concept of building complete and integrated resort cities from 'the ground up' on undeveloped sites. Over a period of several months, the Bank of Mexico conducted a detailed investigation of Mexico's coastline, evaluating several dozen potential sites.

These site studies involved many considerations—land ownership; climatological conditions; environmental impact; types of soil; transportation access; telecommunications; nearby population centres; socio-economic levels of the local population and their past experience in tourism; and other factors. The climatological and related surveys included average hours of sunshine, levels of ocean tides, distribution and strength of prevailing winds, frequency of natural disasters and other characteristics.

Based on the site studies, the Bank of Mexico in early 1969 recommended the creation of five integrated tourist resort cities, each for specific reasons. These resorts are as follows—

- *Cancun (on the Caribbean coast in the state of Quintana Roo)*—selected because of its strategic location in the Caribbean as a region that was already attracting many tourists, its potential for reinforcing the limited existing tourism development on the offshore islands of Cozumel and Isla Mujeres, and to strengthen the regional development of Quintana Roo.
- *Ixtapa (on the Pacific coast in the state of Guerrero)*—selected in order to relieve the tourism concentration in Acapulco which is located about 200 kilometres to the southeast, because of its location near to Zihuatanejo which already had some tourism that would help support marketing of the resort, and to provide impetus for regional development of the state.
- *Los Cabos and Loreto (two sites on the Pacific coast in the southern part of the peninsula of Baja California)*—selected in order to reinforce the limited existing tourism development in that area, publicise this area more to the American market, and stimulate regional economic development alongwith attracting more people to this under-populated region.
- *Bahias de Huatulco (on the Pacific coast in the state of Oaxaca)*—selected because of its great tourism potential and to revitalise the weak economy of Oaxaca.

All these places met the immediate site selection criteria, including good beaches, scenic surroundings, climatic desirability and availability of land for development.

The President then issued a policy statement on the need for encouraging tourism development for its economic benefits. This was immediately followed by the creation in 1969 of the National Fund for Tourism Infrastructure (known by its Spanish acronym of INFRATUR). This agency was organised to implement the following objectives :

- Conceive and implement tourism infrastructure projects that complement investments of the federal government.
- Develop tourism infrastructure project that generate private investment.
- Acquire, develop, sub-divide, sell and lease property associated with tourism projects.
- Collaborate with other government agencies in the promotion of tourism.

INFRATUR was assigned the primary mission of initiating the construction of the first two resorts—Cancun and Ixtapa. The first activity undertaken was to specify the guidelines for the resort development and prepare the resort master plans. These plans are integrated and comprehensive. They included land use zones—for hotels, residential, commercial, public facilities and conservation areas—the transportation network, and the utilities system of water supply, electric power, sewage collection and disposal and telecommunications. In the case of Cancun, an international airport was sited. The Cancun plan includes a large new town for the resort support population, in keeping with the concept of developing resort cities.

The resort plans contain detailed projections and recommendations—characteristics of tourist arrivals; numbers of hotels and hotel rooms; hotel occupancy levels; number of daily air flights expected; and investment procedures. The master plans also establish the quality of construction, building heights, density limits and architectural styles.

The first step in the development process was acquisition of sufficient land for short-medium- and long-term needs. Field work commenced at Cancun in early 1970. One year later the initiation of work at Ixtapa was authorised. The underground infrastructure—water supply and sewer pipes, electric and telephone lines, and drainage—was installed first. Then the above ground infrastructure of roads, the airport (at Cancun), sewage and water treatment plants, streets, etc., was constructed. The infrastructure was designed and developed according to international standards.

At Cancun, INFRATUR did the planning, acquisition of land and construction of basic infrastructure for the new town (Cancun City), located next to and integrated with the beach resort area. Housing at Cancun City was developed largely through the existing programmes of various housing and financing agencies of the national government. INFRATUR carried out an excellent programme for training local inhabitants in construction skills. This included language training in Spanish because many of the Mayans living in the Cancun areas peak only their own language. The agency also implemented a training programme in hotel operations. This eventually became successful in producing several hundred graduates annually.

Concurrent with the development of infrastructure, INFRATUR conducted a promotion campaign to attract investment from the private sector for development of hotels and recreational facilities. The first hotel was opened in Cancun in 1973 and, in 1974, the first hotel opened in Ixtapa.

With the impetus of the successful commencement of these two resorts in 1974 the government upgraded the Department of Tourism to the cabinet level status of State Secretariat. At the same time INFRATUR was merged with the Tourism Guarantee Fund. The new agency was named FONATUR. In addition to acquiring sites and developing the resorts' infrastructure and implementing the plans, FONATUR was given the responsibility of granting loans for hotels and making direct investments in commercial facilities throughout the country. In the mid-1970s, the resorts of Los Cabos and Loreto in Baja California were launched. The government continued giving strong support to development of tourism and, in 1984, the Bahias de Huatulco resort in Oaxaca was started.

Funding for FONATUR is primarily from the institution's own resources. In addition, substantial loans were made by the Inter-American Development Bank and the World Bank, with the first loan granted in 1971 (to INFRATUR). An important concept of this public type investment is that it attracts much private investment. Each peso (the Mexican currency) invested by FONATUR is estimated to attract 10 pesos of private investment. In addition, a programme of co-investment with Mexican and foreign capital has been promoted, chiefly for the construction of the first hotels at each resort. In the 1970s and 1980s, FONATUR financed the great majority of hotels in Mexico (within and outside the five resorts). The agency also maintains direct investment in many tourism enterprises—hotels, restaurants, golf courses and tennis complexes. FONATUR is operating on a financially positive basis, and has continued to meet its obligations in repayment of loans.

The government considers that the resorts have generated substantial economic benefits in their regions. It estimates that each hotel room generates 2.5 jobs directly, and the same number indirectly in the tourism supply sector. The direct resort employees earn, on average, 1.5 times the country's minimum wage. In addition, the resorts' construction, which is still on-going, employs large numbers of people. The infrastructure developed for the resort cities has also stimulated overall regional development.

By the late 1980s, FONATUR estimated that the total hotel room capacity in the five resorts accommodated about a quarter of all tourists visiting Mexico. Development of the resorts continues at present. In the case of Cancun, largest and the most internationally recognised of the five resorts, 112 hotels providing approximately 18,000 hotel rooms were in place by the early 1990s. Cancun has a small convention centre, a championship golf course, retail centres, and a variety of water sports facilities. The type of accommodation varies widely, with 72 beach-front hotels on Cancun Island and another 32 mid-level and budget accommodation enterprises in Cancun City. The city has grown to about 300,000 persons with an ultimate population anticipated to be some 400,000 to 500,000.

The range of accommodation in Cancun allows it to attract a diversity of tourists, including a large proportion of domestic tourists. Although tourists come mostly for beach and marine activities, many also visit the Mayan ruins that are located in the region, as well as important nature conservation areas. The resort has stimulated other tourism development along the Quintana Roo coast and some additional development on the offshore islands.

Conclusions

The resort development strategy for Mexico did not evolve from a comprehensive tourism plan. It was, however, based on identifying problems, establishing objectives, formulating policy and then a strategy for developing a particular form of tourism. The country also has policies for development of other forms of tourism, such as urban and rural tourism.

The concept of developing well planned and integrated resorts was particularly progressive for its time of the late 1960s, when integrated resort development was rather a new idea. The government appreciated that well planned resorts would generate less negative environmental and socio-cultural impacts and offer a much better product for tourists. The government expanded this concept to that of resort cities, which integrate well designed communities for the support population. The fact that Cancun City also has developed some accommodation and other tourist facilities, in addition to the large beach-oriented hotels, reflects the extent of integration. This approach broadens tourist markets because of the greater range of facilities available. It is also advantageous for city residents who can live near their jobs, and participate in ownership and management of smaller-scale facilities and services.

Selecting the resort sites was carried out in a methodical manner, according to specific criteria. The sites selected reflect careful consideration of the immediate environmental and social characteristics, as well as the importance that resorts can play in stimulating regional development. All the regions in which the resorts are situated need the economic impetus which tourism can offer. The resorts were developed on a phased basis. This approach provided the opportunity for the more recent resorts to learn from the experience gained in developing the older resorts. Phasing is also important to maintain a balance between market demand and product development.

In determining the development approach, the government realised the importance of establishing a strong agency—first INFRATUR and then FONATUR—with adequate funding for planning, financing and carrying out development according to the plans and development programme schedules. The responsibilities of this agency were enlarged and streamlined over time to meet the development process needs. It was realised that considerable public expenditure would be required for the construction of infrastructure, as a basis for implementing integrated development and to attract the private investment required. However, this investment is well justified with respect to achieving substantial economic development of the country. Much of this investment can also be recovered over the long-term period.

It is interesting to note that these resorts, in addition to providing a variety of their own recreation and entertainment facilities, also serve as bases for tourists to visit attractions in their regions. This expands the tourism products and markets, and spreads the economic benefits of tourism more widely. These regional relationships reflect the important principle that resorts should be planned and developed within the context of their regions.

From the market standpoint, the Cancun resort has probably attracted some foreign tourists who otherwise would have gone to Caribbean Island destinations. However, this may provide the competitive stimulus for those islands to improve their product. In the case of Cancun, it appears that hotel room rates had to be somewhat lowered in order to attract the large volume of tourists needed to support the hotels.

Inevitably, some problems were encountered in implementing development. These problems were recognised and resolved over a period of time. As concluded by FONATUR, the resort development strategy in Mexico has been economically and environmentally successful. The strategy has greatly assisted the country in commencing to realise its tourism potential.

14

Village Tourism in Senegal

The village tourism programme in Senegal is an example of a national tourism policy applied to effect a particular type of regional tourism development. It is also a good case study of community involvement in tourism that provides exposure of tourists to local life styles and generates benefits directly to local villages.

Background

Senegal is located in West Africa and is the westernmost of all the continental African countries. Geographically, the country is composed mostly of low-lying plains and marshes laced by several rivers. There are some highlands in the far southeast. The separate country of The Gambia occupies the Gambia River area extending through the west-central part of Senegal. The population of more than 7 million is French speaking and mostly Islamic. Dakar, the capital and a major seaport, contains more than 1.2 million inhabitants.

The country offers a variety of attractions for tourists—the cosmopolitan ambience of Dakar with its good hotels and restaurants; several excellent beaches and beach resorts along the coast; the historic slave centre heritage complex on Gorce Island; a large national park with wildlife viewing in the southeast; an important bird sanctuary in the northwest; and the cultural traditions of the people. Also a major attraction is the Casamance region, in the southern part of the country, where village tourism offers the opportunity for exposure to the traditional African way of life in an interesting riverine environment. In the early 1990s, Senegal had about 250,000 tourist arrivals annually, the largest amount of all the West African countries. Most tourists are from Western Europe.

Village Tourism Programme

The village tourism programme was conceived in the early 1970s. (This case study is taken from Tourism for discovery: A project in Lower Casamance, Senegal's by Christian Saglio in the book *Tourism—Passport to Development?* [published for the World Bank and UNESCO by Oxford University Press, 1979], and updated from more recent sources.) Its inception was in response to various concerns being expressed by the government and others during the late 1960s and early 1970s. At that time tourism was based primarily on beach resorts and urban hotels with organised excursions sometimes taken into the countryside. This type of tourism did not offer tourists the opportunity to experience the African way of life and meet Africans on a spontaneous basis. It was also seen by some residents as being socially degrading. Local people often felt that they must meet the expectations of the tourists. They were worried about the demonstration effect of tourists on their young people and the loss of traditional values.

Also there was concern about the need to provide a variety of jobs and income to young people in the villages. Many young villagers were migrating to the cities in order to improve their lives economically. Additionally, the villages needed money to finance community development facilities and services. The village tourism programme was not viewed as the only desirable type of tourism for the country. Rather it was intended to supplement more conventional forms of tourism with an alternative type.

First a model of the village tourism programme was formulated. This called for simple accommodation to be built, managed and operated by the local village people. The lodgings would be designed in the traditional style and built of local materials. They would offer only minimal comforts to small groups of tourists. According to the model, management of the lodgings (called camps) was to be left entirely to the villagers. Cooperatives would be organised to be responsible for the operation of the camps, as well as the allocation of profits. Meals would be planned around the use of local food products and traditional cuisine. The cooperatives would organise tourist activities. Tourist promotion would be based on straightforward descriptions of what the villages had to offer.

The next step was to select a suitable place to commence the project. After many reconnaissance trips were made to examine possible sites in Senegal, the final selection was the Lower Casamance. This region lies between The Gambia and the southern border of the country. It includes the Casamance River and its tributaries. In this region, distances are short, the environment is interesting and the climate is agreeable. The area is well populated. The regional capital already offers comfortable hotel facilities, and a major beach resort was in operation on the coast of the region. These existing tourist facilities would provide a base for tourists to visit and explore the region, staying overnight in the proposed camps.

The project was, and still is, strongly supported by the national and regional governments and tourism offices. Technical advice was provided by an international specialist who had had field experience. The regional coordinator for tourism supervised operations, taking part in all meetings, and encouraging the villagers by making many visits. He also helped run an in-service training programme for the village management teams. An international agency (Canadian University Service Overseas) provided some financial assistance for salaries, an all-terrain vehicle, and travel expenses. Only villages receptive to the project were invited to join it.

The model, as described above, was closely followed in implementation. Four village projects were initially developed. However, some problems were inevitably encountered. During the first year, a serious drought resulted in many people leaving the villages, with a consequent shortage of labour. The remaining workers were distracted by their immediate drought problems, and it was difficult to interest them in the project and train teams for operation and construction.

A second problem related to the major effort required to inform people about the new project and gain their cooperation. Also some local administrative authorities, accustomed to large-scale tourism development, were often suspicious of the project. They criticised the small amount of investment being made, feared problems in the villages, and wondered if tourists would stay in clay houses. There was a reluctance to show visitors some of the traditional life styles, which many of the educated officials tend to believe is backward. Many of both the officials and villagers thought the lodging should be constructed of modern materials and have hotel amenities.

Selecting sites for the lodging was difficult because of rivalries among the village leaders, especially between village heads representing government and the still influential traditional chiefs. These disagreements were resolved only after many meetings and discussions. The sites chosen were deliberately isolated and away form major tourist routes. Access was often only by boat or footpath which presented travel problems. Once a site was selected, a well had to be drilled to provide a water supply. These wells helped win support from the villagers because they provided them with additional water sources. Much effort was put into faithfully reproducing the traditional house styles and arranging for purchase of local building materials. These problems were overcome and, by 1974, the first camp had opened. The initial four camps were completed by 1976.

Management and operation of the camps are carefully organised. Under the authority of the village chief, the work of serving visitors is assigned to young people of the village. A management committee supervises three operating units of two persons each—these units are respectively in charge of meals, accommodation and excursions. Tourist prices are set by agreement, as are the wages of each worker and the share allocated to the cooperative. The employees are paid after each visit according to the number of tourists and the services rendered.

The profits that accrue to the cooperatives are distributed by boards composed of members appointed by the village. These members are typically community leaders. This money is used for community facilities—health and maternity clinics, youth centres and schools. It is also used to initiate new business activities, such as vegetable farming, livestock raising, fishing and crafts. These activities provide more jobs for local young people.

The village tourism programme was an immediate success with rists. Some of the guests staying at the beach resorts take tours of the Casamance and make overnight stays at the camps. Other tourists come for longer stays. In order to diversify the tourist markets, the national tourism office has encouraged several travel agencies to sell tours that include the Casamance camps. Agencies specialising in youth groups arrange for stays of up to three weeks in the camps.

In order to avoid saturation of the camps and villages, which could lead to social problems in the villages and weaken the sense of tourists' contact with villagers, certain size controls have been established. Camps are located in villages with at least 1,000 inhabitants. Accommodation is limited to 20–30 beds in each camp. As more facilities are needed, the existing camps are not expanded, but new ones are build elsewhere in the region.

By the early 1990s, a considerable number of camps have been developed in the Casamance region. These are located in various places north and south of the river with two on the coast. Reservations can be made to stay in the camps through the *Campements Rurals Integres* system. The camps are quite popular and reservations are typically required during the high seasons of July-August and December-January. The success of these camps has stimulated private investment. Attracted by the modest outlay of capital required, ease of construction, and quick return of revenue, several small-scale regional business persons have developed private camps. They are competitive in pricing and are also popular with tourists. However, they may not provide as much revenue to the villages for community development.

Conclusions

The Casamance village tourism project represents a successful approach to developing community-based tourism that directly benefits the villagers, and brings more cultural understanding and interesting experiences to tourists. The success of the programme depended on several factors that can be applied in many other local tourism development projects. The initial careful modelling was essential, even though this was somewhat adapted in application. The strong support of both the national and regional governments was very important. The technical and financial assistance, as well as some dedicated involvement of outside officials, was invaluable. Education of the villagers and local officials was a necessary aspect of implementing the programme. Patience and persistence in pursuing the programme objectives were necessary. The local organisation of labour and finances seemed to work well in this social environment. Use of the profits for community projects and expanding economic activities results in the entire village receiving the benefits of tourism.

The policy of not allowing the camps to become too large in any one village has been a wise choice. The original concept of the programme has been maintained and, by developing new camps, more villages can benefit from the programme. The programme has also served a purpose in stimulating private investment in camps. This has helped reinforce tourism development in the region. Additionally, the Casamance village tourism programme has introduced a new type of tourism product to the country. This has resulted in greater overall tourist flows.

Although successful, continuous monitoring of this type of programme must be pursued. Monitoring will give greater assurance that any problems which arise will be quickly resolved. It also provides a basis for refining techniques which can then be applied to new village tourism projects.

The Casamance programme has evoked much interest from other places in the world, and has served as a model for similar type projects elsewhere. As is always the case, of course, the model must be adapted to the governmental, socio-cultural, economic and environmental situations where it is being applied. This type of programme can result in developing an imaginative new and successful type of tourism that is responsive to certain market demands and brings benefits to local residents.

15

Economic Benefits in the Tibet Tourism

Particular emphasis was given to ways of enhancing economic benefits in the tourism plan for Tibet. This is a good example of the many techniques that can be applied to increase the economic opportunities from tourism.

Background

Tibet is an Autonomous Region of the People's Republic of China, located in south-central Asia north of India, Nepal and Bhutan. The region's southern boundary lies in the Himalaya, where mountains rise to more than 8,000 metres. Much of Tibet occupies a high plateau averaging some 4,000 metres in altitude. The landscape is largely treeless with grasslands in the upper valleys and cultivated fields in the lower valleys. Isolated forests occur on the approaches to the Himalaya. In the southeast, which receives the summer monsoon rains, the grasslands merge into rainforests which contain a diversity of flora and fauna. Despite the high altitude, the climate of southern Tibet is equable, with long hours of sunshine in both the summer and winter.

Most of the population of about 2.2 million inhabit the sheltered valleys, lying between 3,500 and 4,000 metres, which thread the mountainous plateau. Most people live in villages and engage in agriculture and animal husbandry. The capital of Lhasa and the few other towns are situated in this more settled area. Buddhism has been the focus of Tibetan culture for well over 1,000 years. The region has a rich heritage of cultural traditions and historic and religious monuments. Although many of these places were damaged in recent years, much remains and an active restoration programme is underway. People are gradually returning to formerly abandoned monasteries and temples.

Tibet offers both cultural and natural attractions. The villages provide exposure to traditional architecture and life styles. Of the towns, Lhasa and its Potala Palace is by far the most interesting. Many of the historic monuments of monasteries, temples and palaces scattered through the countryside are significant attractions. Traditional dress, customs and festivals comprise important features. Most of southern Tibet is scenically and environmentally interesting, and provides opportunities for trekking and sightseeing. There is much potential for developing mountaineering along the northern franks of the Himalaya, with 22 peaks legally open (in 1990) to foreign expeditions. More generally, the mystique of Tibet holds a fascination for many tourists.

Tibet was first opened to foreign tourists in 1980, and a peak of 43,500 tourist arrivals was reached in 1987. Because of civil strife in the late 1980s, the number of arrivals greatly decreased, but again picked up to an estimated 8,500 in 1990. Most tourists come from Western Europe with lesser numbers from the USA, Japan and Australia. The majority of tourists are independent travellers and the remainder come on group tours. The authorised tourist hotels are considered to provide satisfactory accommodation. Access to the region is by air to Lhasa from where transportation is by road to other parts of the country. The road network is being improved but access to many attraction places is still difficult. Other infrastructure is limited. The marked decrease of tourist arrivals in the late 1980s resulted in considerable excess capacity of accommodation and a surplus of tourism employees.

Tourism Planning Approach

The regional tourism plan for Tibet was prepared in 1990 (UNDP and WTO, 1990. *Tourism Plan for Tibet Autonomous Region, People's Republic of China,* Madrid: WTO). This is a comprehensive plan that examines all the elements of tourism. It recommends a development concept, improvements required to accommodation and other tourist facilities, services and infrastructure, and a marketing strategy. Economic, social and environmental impacts are evaluated. Implementation policies are recommended on procedural and technical issues—the institutional framework for tourism; development of key tourism services; development of economic opportunities; and manpower development and training. A detailed development programme for 1991–95 is recommended. Physical plans are presented for various demonstration projects including an improvement plan for Lhasa. Design guidelines for development of tourist facilities are recommended in the plan.

The plan proposes market targets by five-year periods up to 2010. For that year a total of 170,000 arrivals are targeted. These targets are composed of about three-quarters general interest tourists, and the remainder are trekkers and a small number of mountaineers. Source markets would continue being primarily Western Europe, the USA and Japan.

The development concept of the plan is focused on the coordinated realisation of the tourism potential of the cultural, historic and environmental resources which are special to Tibet. It emphasises the consolidation and further development of those cultural features and tourist activities which currently attract tourists. At the same time, new attractions of a different type should be opened up to widen the appeal of Tibet to general and special interest groups. The concept defines several tourism zones, each with distinctive characteristics suitable for different touristic pursuits. The major zones are linked by a system of touring circuits to facilitate visits to a wide range of destinations offering a variety of experiences.

The plan designates three cultural zones—one primary zone (focused on Lhasa), one secondary zone, and the third zone being of minor importance to general interest tourists. Four trekking areas are defined, with trekking routes shown on the plan. Two environmental zones are designated. These are areas of outstanding environmental quality, based on their scenic beauty and wealth of flora and fauna, with particular appeal to general interest tourists for relaxation and recreation. The projected accommodation rooms needed are allocated to the various zones.

Touring circuits are defined in the plan as circular road routes which link a number of destinations and take tourists several days to accomplish. Stopovers are made at different laces along the route. Three touring circuits are recommended, with possible combinations of these for the longer-stay tourists. The plan examines the potential for developing mountaineering, pony trekking, white-water rafting and mountain biking. Ways to give tourists greater exposure to the Tibetan culture are suggested—organised presentations of song and dance; exhibitions in museums; and visits to villages, nomadic camps and traditional festivals.

In the marketing strategy, the plan indicates that the initial step is to establish an image of Tibet as a viable tourist destination. The strategy emphasises that a programme must be instituted for removal of constraints on marketing, improving the tourism product and informing the world of these changed circumstances. Image-building would then focus on establishing Tibet as a mystery land of scenic beauty, great mountains and old monasteries, peopled by agriculturalists and nomadic herdsmen. Promotion should be primarily through selected tour operators and travel agents.

Development of Economic Opportunities

An important element of the Tibet tourism planning project was to propose ways in which the present and future economic benefits of tourism could be increased to the local population. The plan includes a section on development of economic opportunities, in addition to conducting the standard economic impact analysis of tourism. This element is given emphasis because of Tibet's present economic underdevelopment and low income of the population. The plan points out that, although Tibet has considerable natural resources, their development is difficult because of the huge size of the region, its mountainous geography and small population. The relatively few number of people provides only a limited local market for manufactured goods.

The plan points out that the general opportunities for economic development in Tibet are mainly in the fields of agriculture, animal husbandry, forestry and minerals, plus tourism. Development of tourism can provide substantial foreign exchange for the region and help diversify the economy. It can create new markets for local products and services. Tourism will also act as a catalyst and help pay for the improvement of infrastructure which will benefit the total economy.

The plan sets forth an economic strategy for tourism, as follows :

- Given the large investment and excess capacity in tourist accommodation, aim in the short-term to increase tourist numbers and length of stay as fast as possible, but without jeopardising the reputation for quality and future sustainable growth.
- Given the limited capital available for investment and the limited infrastructure, minimise the capital costs of developing tourist facilities.
- Maintain prices and value in relation to revenue above the levels of competitors to reflect Tibet's premium status and to maximise revenues, subject to the need to improve the reputation for quality of services.
- Increase the length of stay of tourists.
- Increase retail and incidental spending per tourist which, with increasing the length of stay, offers the greatest potential for increasing revenues.

Improving regional economic linkages, resulting in greater use of local products and services, is also identified as an important means of enhancing local economic benefits.

For increasing the number of tourist arrivals during the near-term period, the plan makes several recommendations—more promotion of tourism, some reduction in prices, improvements in quality of services, and relaxation of restrictions on independent travellers. The plan states that it will be difficult to reach the market targets solely from group tours, and independent travel should also be encouraged. The plan emphasises that a substantial increase in the average length of stay can be achieved only by developing new activities and locations. This will require new investment. Trekking, however, offers the potential to develop new activities at a relatively low cost and should be expanded rapidly.

In order to minimise the capital investment costs of tourism development, the plan recommends :

- Coordinating the development of tourist facilities with infrastructure improvements.

- Making the best use of existing facilities, for example, upgrading the Tibetan (locally owned) hotels rather than building new hotels.
- Not providing costly facilities for seasonal peak demands, and choosing low cost solutions for seasonal use, such as tented camps, where appropriate.
- Once capacity of facilities is reached in the peak months, focus efforts on increasing occupancy at other times through pricing and promotion before investing in additional capacity.

When capital resources are needed, the plan indicates that they can be drawn from the central government, profits of existing tourism enterprises, local bank loans and international sources.

On pricing of facilities and services, the plan recommends that present premium prices be maintained (except for a slight reduction to attract more tourists), as a means of increasing tourism income. As Tibet becomes better known, it will have to offer more competitive prices.

The plan indicates that raising the spending per tourist can be encouraged in various ways. The range of goods available for tourists should be expanded, including imported goods where necessary. The items related to Tibetan culture, such as handicrafts and books, can be increased for sale to tourists. Tourists can be allowed more opportunities in their itineraries for retail shopping and incidental spending.

On improving regional economic linkages, the plan makes several recommendations :

- Use local materials, to the extent possible, in the construction of hotels and other tourist facilities.
- Increase the production of local food items used in tourism. Opportunities exist especially for local production of poultry, eggs, milk products, bakery goods and fresh vegetables.
- Expand the production and sales of locally produced handicrafts through extending the range of items produced, adapting designs to tourists' tastes, and establishing training programmes in craft skills and quality controls. Some assistance will be needed to expand local production of crafts.

- Provide more supplies and services for trekking, including fresh and processed food items and some equipment such as Tibetan style tents.

Conclusions

The planning approach of the Tibet tourism plan is comprehensive, with particular attention given to priority issues. The development concept applies the principle of establishing tourism zones for different types of tourism areas. Additionally, the plan recommends tourism circuits for sightseeing tourists. These circuits are related to the tourism zones.

The emphasis given to development of local economic opportunities reflects the concern that tourism should generate maximum benefits to Tibetans. The plan's proposals for expanding these opportunities include ones which are applicable in many places—attracting more tourists in the near future in order to make use of existing excess capacity of tourist facilities; increasing the length of stay of tourists; making effective use of limited capital resources; maintaining high pricing levels; increasing spending per tourist; and improving regional economic linkages. However, they have been adapted to the Tibetan situation so that they are more likely to be effective.

An interesting approach recommended is that of not providing costly facilities only for peak season use, because this does not make effective use of capital resources. Rather, the plan recommends that seasonality be reduced through promotion and pricing techniques, and that low cost facilities such as tented camps be used to absorb the extra need during the peak season.

Some of the recommendations made, such as locally producing more food items and handicrafts, will require detailed programming, developing some pilot projects and technical and financial assistance. Attention will also need to be given to effective marketing of these products. However, experience with application of these approaches elsewhere indicates that such investments can be very worthwhile in increasing local production.

16

Management of Tourism in the Maldives

Tourism development has been carefully managed in the Maldives so that it does not generate any serious environmental or social problems, while still making a major contribution to the economy. This has been achieved through careful planning and application of strict controls.

Background

The Republic of Maldives is situated southwest of India and west of Sri Lanka in the Indian Ocean. The country is composed of 26 atolls containing about 1,200 low-lying islands spread over a north-south distance of approximately 800 kilometers. About 200 islands are inhabited. The total population is somewhat more than 200,000, with about 50,000 living in the capital city of Male. The society is Islamic, and religious values and customs are strictly maintained. There is a single local language. Natural resources are limited and the economy is based mostly on fishing and tourism.

The primary attractions for tourists in the Maldives are the warm, sunny tropical climate, scenic island beauty and activities related to the extensive beach and marine environment. Snorkelling and scuba diving are especially popular. Tourism commenced in 1972, when two resorts were opened and about 1,000 tourists visited the islands. In 1990, there were nearly 200,000 tourist arrivals. The major tourist markets are Western European countries. The Japanese market is also becoming important. The average length of stay of tourists is about nine days. International tourism receipts constitute the single most important source of foreign exchange for the country, and tourism contributes about 20 per cent to the Gross National Product. There is a high import content of goods used in tourism.

The physical configuration of tourism development in the Maldives is an unusual one. Virtually all development is composed of resorts, about 75 of them, which vary in size from six to more than 150 rooms. Each resort occupies a separate island and is totally self-contained. The resort islands are accessible only by boat from the international airport, also on its own island. The capital of Male extends over another entire island. The majority of resorts are developed in Kaafu Atoll where Male and the airport are located. There are some resorts on other atolls, mostly on Alif Atoll situated west of Kaafu.

A tourism plan prepared for the Maldives in the early 1980s provided some ideas for development. However, most of the tourism planning and environmental management for the country has resulted from government initiatives, based on its evaluation of the best forms and standards of development. (The material in this case study is taken from information provided by the Maldives government, other publications and field observations.) Many of the government's present approaches and standards have evolved through monitoring of the earlier phases of development to determine what is most suitable. Approaches and standards are refined—and some may be discarded—based on the experience gained from previous types of development.

Planning of Tourism Development

The Ministry of Tourism (then a department) was organised in 1978. The Ministry has been very active in guiding the growth of tourism and applying strict development and operating standards on new and existing resorts. The Ministry, for example, has the power to close substandard resorts if, after imposing fines, operating standards have not been improved. One of its important functions is to formulate and implement environmental protection policies and regulations. The coral island and reef ecosystem is extremely fragile, and the government recognises that both fishing and tourism are dependent upon preservation of this ecosystem. The Ministry also coordinates closely with the private sector. It regularly holds meetings with the resort owners and managers, tour operators and others involved in tourism.

By government policy, the resorts are located on uninhabited islands, in order to reduce any possible socio-cultural impacts. Also most islands are too small to contain both resorts and traditional villages. These islands are owned by the government and it can allocate them for resort use as needed. The resort developer receives a long-term lease and pays an annual rent that is calculated individually for each island. The resorts must provide their own infrastructure of electric power, water supply, sewage and solid waste disposal, boat dock and recreation facilities. They must also provide housing and related facilities for the resort employees. The families of employees remain on their home islands, often some distance away.

The government policy has been to expand tourism for its economic benefits, but in a systematic manner of staged development. In the late 1980s, Kaafu Atoll was considered saturated with resort development. This decision was made within the framework of maintaining high environmental standards for the existing resorts, and retaining sufficient land for village and urban expansion and recreation parks. In fact, one of the older resorts located near Male city is being phased out to allow for development of a satellite community of Male, to absorb urban expansion of the capital.

All new resort development is programmed to take place in Alif Atoll, which is accessible by boat from the international airport. In 1988, 16 islands in Alif were designated for resort development. These were allocated to developers based on approval of their development plans, financial arrangements and other considerations. By the early 1990s, most of these new resorts had been developed. During this period of expansion in Alif, no new resorts are allowed elsewhere in the country.

Additionally, the government policy is to encourage upgrading of existing older resorts to higher standards, including meeting present environmental quality standards. This upgrading is considered necessary to maintain the viability and competitiveness of these resorts. Also the aim is to maintain all tourism development at a reasonably high quality level, catering to quality tourist markets. Much of this upgrading has been accomplished.

Because of limited availability of local financial resources, the government encourages foreign investment as needed. As the country develops, especially the tourism sector, there will be a greater amount of local capital available for investment.

Environmental Standards and Controls

As an important basis for deciding the number of rooms and extent of resort facility development allowed on each resort island, the government has established carrying capacity standards. These are based on several factors :

- Control of tree cutting so that the natural appearance and facade of the island are maintained with no buildings allowed to appear above the tree tops.
- The maximum island area to be occupied by buildings is 20 per cent, with two-storey buildings allowed to conserve land area if there is sufficient vegetation to conceal these buildings from the ocean view. Equal space will be left open on the island for every building developed on the lagoon. (Based on the experience of actual development, buildings on the lagoon are not now being encouraged.)
- In order to preserve the tourists' perception and image of beach orientation, all guest rooms should be facing the beach, with a minimum of 5 metres of linear beach available in front of each room. Sixty-eight per cent of the total length of beach on the island is allocated for guest room frontage, 20 per cent for general resort facilities and the remaining 12 per cent left as open space.

The exact capacity of each resort island is decided after reviewing the proposed resort layout, and determining how well the plan meets the above guidelines and fits into the overall environment.

For environmental protection, the government applies various measures. These include the following :

- *Architectural control of resort buildings*—so that they are well integrated into the island environment, take advantage of the tropical climate and use local building materials, such as thatch roofs, to the extent possible. Previously many buildings of all types were constructed from coral stone mined from the reefs. However, the mining of coral is now restricted to a few isolated reefs in order to prevent any further environmental damage to the remaining reefs. The use of imported building materials is now being encouraged, although these are expensive by local standards.

- *Controls on the heights of buildings*—no more than two storeys.
- *Setbacks of buildings from the shoreline*—a minimum of 5 metres, with suitable landscaping to complement the natural vegetation.
- *Design of boat piers*—in such a manner that they do not result in beach erosion or deposition. Previously, solid-based piers were developed which led to some environmental problems. Now piers must be built on pilings with free flow of water under the piers.
- *Provision of adequate potable water supply*—usually a combination of restricted use of the limited groundwater, roof catchment and storage, and desalination using the reverse osmosis technique.
- *Provision of proper sewage disposal systems*—the actual system used will depend largely on the size of the resort.
- *Provision of proper solid waste disposal systems*—utilising controlled incineration, compaction and disposal in deep water sea areas. Empty cans must be compressed and plastic materials cannot be disposed in the sea. Recycling of some waste material is being experimented with, but this requires shipping the material outside the country.
- *Encouragement given to undergrounding utility lines*—installation of overhead lines is discouraged.
- *Controls on the marine ecology*—prohibition of collection of coral, seashells and even rocks from the sea, reefs and beaches and use of harpoons and guns to kill fish (spear-fishing) by tourists; and prohibition of purchase by the resorts of turtles and tortoises under a certain size and young lobsters and female lobsters ready to lay eggs. Sport fishing by tourists with lines and hooks is permitted.
- *Controls on turtle products*—prohibition of the display and sale of stuffed turtles and tortoises in shops and the export of turtle and tortoise shells and black coral in whole form. Ornaments made out of these materials are allowed to be produced, sold to tourists and exported.

There are plans to establish marine conservation areas or reserves where more stringent environmental controls would be applied. For the safety of tourists, the government applies strict regulations on wind surfing and diving operations. Resorts are required to employ internationally qualified diving instructors and dive masters. These may be Maldivians who have passed international examinations.

Socio-cultural and Economic Considerations

Several policies and controls have been established which relate to socio-cultural and economic considerations. Islamic codes and customs are carefully maintained. Nude bathing is prohibited and fines are imposed on both the bather and resort management if this regulation is violated. Tourists visiting inhabited islands for picnics or excursions are not allowed to go swimming on those islands. Locally acceptable dress codes must be observed by tourists when they visit Male or the island villages.

Cruises for tourists can be conducted only in atolls where tourist facilities are available and tourists are not allowed to visit other atolls. The atolls approved for visits are listed by the government. Tour groups can be taken to certain traditional villages on a prearranged basis for sightseeing and to purchase local handicrafts made in those villages. These regulations have been respected by tourists and resort management, with very few exceptions.

With permission, alcoholic beverages can be imported and served in the resorts. However, Maldivian employees are not allowed to handle and serve these beverages. Most bartenders are from Sri Lanka. Maldivian employees (except waiters and other employees required to do specific work) and Maldivian visitors to the resorts are prohibited from entering the bars and shops where liquor is sold. Maldivians, foreign employees and tourists are not allowed to carry liquor with them when leaving the resort islands. No pork is produced in the islands, and pork may be imported, by permit, only for consumption in the resorts. Pork dishes must be labelled when served in buffets. It is prohibited for pork to be sold, given or served to Maldivians.

The ensure that Maldivians, and especially the urban residents of Male, have sufficient recreation facilities, an island in Kaafu Atoll near Male has been designated and developed as a recreation park for Maldivians. This park is quite popular with the Maldivians on weekends and holidays. A similar island recreation park is being developed in Alif Atoll for use by the residents there. The land areas of these island parks are limited, and therefore they can be visited by tourists only on days when there is little demand for use by Maldivians.

Preference must be given to Maldivians for employment in resorts. Work permits for expatriate employees are granted only for bartenders and others who have special skills not yet available locally. Through education, training and experience, Maldivians are commencing to assume higher level technical and managerial positions in the resorts.

Because most fruits and vegetables must be imported for resort use, one larger resort has taken the initiative to develop a hydroponic farm. This has been successful in supplementing the resort's needs for certain imported vegetables. A chicken farm has been established to provide some locally produced poultry, although its production costs have been higher than imported poultry. Locally caught fish and other sea food items are used extensively in the resort menus, as are some locally grown fruits. Beef and pork must be imported.

The resorts must provide suitable housing, community and religious facilities and services for the employees who live on the resort islands. These are typically located in the interior of the islands. The fact that those employees who work in resorts located some distance from their home islands may see little of their families does not seem to cause any serious problems.

The Ministry of Tourism has implemented a public education programme to inform Maldivians about tourism. The programme emphasises the economic importance of tourism, and attempts to raise the environmental awareness of Maldivians. This education programme is conducted in the public school system and on the radio, the islands' primary communications medium. The local television station also includes news items about tourism.

Traditionally not attuned to structured regular employment, more Maldivians are being attracted to work in tourism. By policy, the government encourages Maldivian employment in tourism in order to reduce the previously high rates of unemployment and underemployment, increase income levels, and decrease the number of foreign employees. At the same time, some concern is being expressed that, over the long-term, tourism should not deplete the labour supply necessary to maintain the fisheries industry, the other major sector of the economy.

Training persons to work in tourism is being promoted. A hotel and catering school, assisted by the WTO, UNDP and European Community, was opened in Male in 1987 and is operating successfully. Also, several of the government tourism staff have been involved in internationally sponsored local and overseas tourism management education. Some of the hotel staff are sent overseas for training by the larger resorts.

Conclusions

The Maldives have developed a very suitable form of tourism—it is appropriate for their small-island environment; does not generate any serious environmental or socio-cultural impacts; creates substantial economic benefits; and meets tourist expectation and satisfaction levels. It is interesting to note that this has been accomplished through government commitment initiatives and application of strict regulations over a period of time. Success has been based on government policy, but not a particular tourism plan. The techniques applied by the Maldives government in developing sustainable tourism, however, are those which tourism planners typically use in their plans for island destinations.

Many of the present environmentally suitable standards in the Maldives have resulted from experimentation with various approaches—discarding those which were seen to be unsuitable, and adopting and refining those which were deemed to be appropriate. A wise move, in recent years, has been upgrading of the older resorts and ensuring that new resorts meet good quality standards. The Maldives have thus become a 'quality' destination. With respect to demands on the reef system from both general development and tourism, several appropriate measures have been taken, but continued monitoring of any further reef deterioration will need to be maintained.

Much of the effectiveness of the approach in the Maldives has derived from having a competent government tourism office, with a good working relationship and coordination established between the public and private sectors. This public-private sector cooperation is one which is always encouraged in contemporary tourism management. Success has also been assisted by other factors—a strong central government; a homogeneous population with a single set of religiously-based social values; and government control of land.

With respect to socio-cultural considerations, a minor issue is the separation of many of the men working in the resorts (most resort employees are men) from their families and communities. However, employees are allowed to visit their home villages during the Moslem fasting month of Ramadan (foreign workers are employed during that period). The government is investigating the possibilities of developing complete new communities on uninhabited islands located near to resorts, where employees can live with their families and commute to work by boat. Also, a consideration to be made in the future is whether, within the framework of Maldivian Islamic values, to encourage more women to work in the resorts.

An economic issue is the extent to which goods must be imported for use in tourism. Efforts are being made to produce more items locally, but the Maldives have very limited resources and few manufacturing industries. It will not likely be possible to achieve complete import substitution. Even with a high import content, however, tourism still brings substantial benefits to the society.

The government recognises that it will need to decide whether and how much to expand tourism in the future. It wishes to maintain a diversified economy based on both tourism and fisheries. It also does not want to encourage any more migration of foreign workers. If tourism is developed to the extent hat tourism depletes the local labour supply, to the detriment of maintaining fishing activities, the economy will become too dependent on a single economic sector.

17

Management in Tibet Tourism

The Tibet tourism plan includes an assessment of environmental and social impacts. Various suitable policies and control measures are recommended to manage impacts, including a Tourist Code of Conduct.

Background

The background of tourism planning in Tibet was described in a previous case study, and so is only summarised here. Tibet is an Autonomous Region of the People's Republic of China located in south-central Asia. The southern boundary of the country lies in the Himalaya Mountains. Much of Tibet is composed of a high plateau of grasslands averaging some 4,000 metres in altitude. Most of the population of 2.2 million live in villages situated in the sheltered valleys on this plateau. The capital of Lhasa and the few other towns are also located in these valleys. Some forests lie on the approaches to the Himalaya and in the southeastern part of the country. Despite the high altitude, the climate of southern Tibet is equable with long hours of sunshine in both the summer and winter. The region's economy is based primarily on cultivated agriculture and animal husbandry.

The cultural attractions for tourists in Tibet are the traditional patterns of the villages and towns, and many religious and historic monuments of monasteries, temples and palaces. Buddhism has been the focus of Tibetan culture farewell over 1,000 years. The natural attractions relate to scenic beauty and environmentally interesting areas that offer opportunities for trekking, mountain climbing and sightseeing. Tibet was first opened to tourists in 1980 with a peak of 43,500 arrivals reached in 1987. Because of civil strife, tourism sharply dropped in the late 1980s and then picked up somewhat to an estimated 8,500 arrivals in 1990. Access to the region is by air to Lhasa, and from there by road to other parts of the country. Most authorised tourist accommodation is considered to be satisfactory. Infrastructure is limited and some attraction areas are not easily accessible.

The regional tourism plan for Tibet was prepared in 1990 (UNDP and WTO, 1990. *Tourism Plan for Tibet Autonomous Region, People's Republic of China.* Madrid: WTO). This is a comprehensive plan that examines all aspects of tourism. The market targets established indicate a substantial growth of tourism over a 20-year period. About three-quarters of these tourists will be of the general interest type and the remainder will be trekkers and mountaineers. The development concept in the plan is focused on coordinated realisation of the tourism potential of those cultural, historic and environmental resources which are special to Tibet. Present attractions will be improved and new ones developed. The plan designates three cultural tourism zones, two zones of environmental interest, and four trekking areas. Three touring circuits are recommended. The near-term marketing strategy focuses on image-building and selective promotion.

Environmental Impact Assessment

The plan considers the impact of tourism on both the man-made and natural environment. Based on the market targets and expected distribution of tourists, the average number of daily visitors to historic monuments is calculated. The plan concludes that these numbers of visitors will not likely exceed the monuments visitor carrying capacities. The example is given of Potala Palace in Lhasa, which will receive the largest number of tourists—about 600 daily during peak periods. This level of use will not congest the palace, although a better means of access will need to be devised.

The plan explains that the development of tourism could possibly cause damage to the natural environment in four principal ways :

- Ecologically sensitive areas may be subjected to greater pressure by being opened up for tourist visits and activities.

- In less sensitive areas, the introduction of relatively large numbers of people on defined routes or at specific places (engaging in activities such as trekking and mountaineering) may cause a general degradation of the immediate environment, and generate large quantities of refuse and sanitation problems.
- The penetration of roads into previously inaccessible forest areas may encourage settlement to take place on slash and burn principles—removal of vegetation for cultivated agriculture—or the commercial extraction of timber.
- Erosion could arise as a consequence of building operations and the construction of roads in mountainous areas of heavy rainfall.

The plan states that the last point is mainly a matter of ensuring good design that takes into account the characteristics of the environment. The other points are reviewed with respect to the tourism zones designated in the plan—the two zones of environmental interest and the four trekking areas.

Calculation of the peak daily use in the environmental zones indicates that the numbers of tourists using these zones at any one time will be relatively small—600 and 850 respectively in each of the zones. Therefore, there will not be any immediate problems associated with overuse. However, in the smaller zone, capacity may be reached by 2005, and environmental impact there should be carefully monitored. The improvement of access roads and tracks in these zones is not considered to generate any negative impacts, if they are properly designed. However, the plan recommends that cutting of timber, except for domestic use such as fuel and housing, should be prohibited in these zones. To accomplish this, the zones should be declared as natural protection areas under environmental conservation legislation.

The two potential environmental problems of trekking and mountaineering—ecological damage from overuse and poor disposal of refuse—are examined. Because of the plan's development strategy of spreading trekking over various large areas, the use of each track will be limited and general environmental damage is not considered likely to be a problem. However, there could be damage from removal of rare plants, the cutting of vegetation for fuel and the grazing of pack animals on the thinly grassed upland areas. The latter two could lead to erosion and resentment among the nomadic people and local residents.

The plan recommends that collection of all plants by tourists be prohibited, in order to ensure that rare plants are not removed. The cutting of firewood by trekking groups should also be prohibited, with use of portable fuel such as kerosene made obligatory. This rule could be relaxed in densely forested areas. Tourist groups should be required to carry sufficient fodder for their pack animals in any area where there is a danger of depleting local supplies or creating erosion conditions.

The plan indicates that refuse disposal is a particularly difficult problem in remote areas. A couple of places are already becoming seriously polluted by refuse that has been discarded by trekkers and mountaineers. The plan suggests that either of two approaches could be used. One is that refuse bins be placed along the trails and at camp sites. The refuse would be periodically removed for disposal in an acceptable manner. The other approach would be to require trekkers to carry out their refuse or to bury it in pits of sufficient depth. The present practice of covering refuse with rocks should to be allowed. Also, as an important measure, both the trekkers and their Tibetan staffs should be educated not to litter trails and camp sites. The plan states that littering of mountaineering camps and trails must also be controlled.

For sanitation, the plan recommends that use of toilet tents and pit latrines should be required for all trekking groups. At more intensively used places permanent sanitary facilities should be developed. Detailed designs for these facilities are illustrated in the plan.

It is recommended that design standards for tourist facilities reflect Tibetan styles and make use of local building materials. This will help integrate the facilities better into the cultural and natural environment, thus lessening their environmental impact.

Tourist Code of Conduct

The plan states that tourists' activities should be regulated by a Code of Conduct to be observed by trekkers, mountaineers and any visitors who journey into the open country for such purposes as picnicking. The recommended code is summarised as follows :

- Not to kill any animal, except under licence, nor cut or remove any growing plant for fuel, except in exempt areas, or for any other purpose.
- Not to damage growing crops nor to harass domestic animals.
- Not to pollute any river, stream, spring or other source of water.
- Not to dispose of any litter, refuse or other items except in authorised refuse containers or in pits dug in accordance with the regulations.
- Not to dispose of human wastes except in accordance with established sanitary procedures.
- Not to permit the grazing of pack animals, except in exempt areas.

This code should be distributed to every tourist, and especially those going trekking or mountaineering. The responsibility for policing the code should be placed with the Tibetans who accompany the tourists as guides, organisers or liaison officers. As part of their training, they should be instructed on how to enforce the code in an effective but tactful manner. The local government authorities would be responsible for maintaining refuse containers.

The plan recommends that all trekkers be required to obtain a trekking permit. The permit fees should be established at a level that will pay for the cost of maintaining trails, collecting and disposing of refuse, and servicing the sanitary facilities. The money collected from permit fees should be specifically allocated for these purposes.

Social Impact Considerations

The plant reviews possible social impacts from tourism. It concludes that there will not be any substantial negative impacts because of the relatively modest level of tourism proposed and the strong Buddhist-based cultural values of Tibetans. The plan points out that there are now many outside influences on the Tibetan culture, in addition to tourism. However, it indicates that there will undoubtedly be some influence by tourists on the Tibetans' attitudes, values and ways of life. Also in the tourism areas, some moderate problems will likely arise—non-traditional begging by children from tourists; petty theft; prostitution; and overly aggressive selling of items by vendors to tourists.

The plan recommends that there be a public education programme about tourism—its nature, benefits and problems—using television and other media, and organising annual tourism weeks. Tourism education programmes should also be included in the public school system at the primary, lower middle and second middle levels. These school programmes would include giving students information about job opportunities in tourism. Teachers will need to have some special training in tourism studies in order to implement this programme. The plan also recommends that tourists be informed about the local culture and possible social problems, and asked to refrain from encouraging begging or to place temptation in the way of petty thieves. Tourists should also be sensitised about adopting proper behavioural patterns at religious places.

Conclusions

The Tibet plan systematically identifies the types of environmental impacts that may result from tourism. This provides a logical basis for recommending preventative measures. A basic policy approach is to spread tourism throughout various places in the region, within the framework of the designated tourism zone. Thus, no one area or specific place becomes overcrowded with tourists, which could lead to serious environmental or social problems. The plan uses a quantitative approach in calculating peak period daily use by tourists, and relates that to carrying capacities. This provides a sound basis for evaluating whether overuse will likely take place. In one area where there might be an excess of tourists in the future, the plan justifiably recommends that environmental impacts be monitored and future development be controlled.

In order to reduce environmental problems along trekking trails and at camp sites, the plan recommends specific environmental control techniques—proper refuse disposal and sanitation, prohibition of tree cutting; and control of use of the local grasslands by pack animals. These are regulations which have been successfully applied elsewhere, for example, in Nepal and other mountain tourism areas. Proposing a Tourist Code of Conduct incorporating these regulations is a very useful technique. This gives responsibility to the tourists and their Tibetan entourage for applying and enforcing the regulations. The requirement for trekkers to obtain permits with the fees used for maintenance of the trekking areas is a reasonable approach which has worked well in other places.

The plan also notes that some environmental problems are being caused by misuse of the landscape by local residents. It recommends the sound approach of designating environmentally important areas for environmental protection, but with controlled private use allowed to continue in these places.

The plan identifies the likely social impacts of tourism, indicating that these should not become serious. It makes the important point that there are various outside influences on the Tibetan society, of which tourism is only one type. The development concept of spreading tourism throughout different areas in the region is very valid for social, as well as environmental, reasons. This reduces the number of tourists and possible adverse social impacts in any one place. The dispersal approach also spreads more widely the economic and social benefits of tourism.

The plan recommends carrying out public education programmes about tourism—including incorporating tourism studies in the public school system—and informing tourists about the local culture and how to behave in their interaction with Tibetans. These are basic approaches which are always important to apply in tourism areas. The next steps would be to organise and implement specific public awareness programmes utilising local communications media, write and distribute teaching guides on tourism to be used in the school system, and prepare and have available for distribution a tourist information brochure.

18

Tourism in Nusa Tenggara

The socio-cultural analysis, policies and programme component of the regional tourism plan for Nusa Tenggara reflect an effective approach to achieve selective cultural conservation, reduce negative impacts and integrate tourism into the local societies.

Background

Nusa Tenggara is located in southeastern Indonesia, east of Java and Bali. It is composed of the two provinces of Nusa Tenggara Barat and Nusa Tenggara Timur. The region includes numerous islands, the largest of which are Lombok, Sumbawa, Flores, Sumba and the western part of Timor. The islands are topographically rugged, with steep-sided mountains, valleys and some coastal and inland plains. Along the coasts are numerous beaches and offshore coral reefs. The climate is tropical with a monsoonal rainy season that varies appreciably from one place to another.

The vegetation is tropical but not jungle, with savanna landscapes of grasslands and scattered trees prevailing in the eastern islands. Nusa Tenggara lies immediately east of the Wallace Line which divides the Asian and Australian types of flora and fauna, although there is considerable overlap of these two types. The most famous animal of the region is the Komodo Dragon, a giant monitor lizard whose main habitat on Komodo Island has been designated and developed as a national park.

The population of Nusa Tenggara is somewhat over 6 million. Several cultural groups live in the region. Each one has its own language, customs and building styles. The cultural patterns of these ethnic groups are based on principles of mythological thinking, in which the sense of belonging to a collective group and family kinship is very strong. In most islands, traditional beliefs have been overlain by the Islamic and Christian religions, but there are some isolated Animist villages. These cultural groups vary in their degree of openness to outside cultural contact and attitudes. This openness also varies greatly between the urban and rural areas.

In the early 1980s, when the plan was prepared, modern development was in its early stages in the region. Tourism was not developed to any great extent, except for limited facilities on Lombok Island where some tourists would visit from nearby Bali. A relatively small number of special interest groups and individual tourists toured the other islands. Basic accommodation existed in the towns for use mostly by business and government travellers.

Nusa Tenggara contains both natural and cultural tourist attractions. The most important specific natural feature is Komodo National Park. Also of much interest are the three coloured crater lakes in central Flores. Other natural attractions include good beach and marine environments—which offer possibilities for development of beach resorts—scenic beauty and opportunities for mountain hiking and camping. Cultural attractions relate to some highly traditional villages and their distinctive layouts and architectural styles, and the traditional dress, music, dance and ceremonies of the various cultural groups. The best developed handicraft is textile weaving, including tie-dye textiles, produced in the traditional manner. Each cultural area has its unique type of the textiles, many of which are internationally known among textile connoisseurs.

Socio-cultural Analysis, Policies and Programme

A comprehensive regional tourism development plan was prepared for Nusa Tenggara in 1981 (UNDP and WTO, 1981. *Tourism Development Plan for Nusa Tenggara, Indonesia.* Madrid: WTO). This planning study includes a major socio-cultural component prepared by an Indonesian development sociologist on the planning team. The objectives for developing tourism in the region incorporate a statement on socio-cultural considerations, as follows :

> Promote the conservation of traditional cultural patterns and their artistic expressions and places of specific historic and cultural

importance which represent the heritage of Nusa Tenggara; and minimise any adverse impact of tourism on the traditional cultures and the general society through carefully controlled development.

The socio-cultural patterns of the region were carefully analysed relative to tourism development. Field trips were made to many places and the existing literature on the various cultural groups was reviewed. As stated in the plan report, socio-cultural considerations in tourism include :

- *Traditional aspects of the Nusa Tenggara cultures*—their unique characteristics which provide attractions for tourists and a sense of cultural identity to the people.
- *The historically isolated nature of the cultures*—although politically and religiously influenced by early contacts of Portuguese, Dutch and Islamic cultures, Nusa Tenggara did not undergo rapid change until national independence. Change and modern influences are taking place in a non-selective manner, especially among young people, with a loss of some traditional patterns and sense of cultural heritage.
- *Constraints imposed by Christian and Islamic religions*—many traditional ceremonies and other cultural elements associated with Animist beliefs are being lost. There is a need to separate traditional elements from religious beliefs so that some aspects of traditional culture can be maintained.

The plan states that tourism will result in both positive and negative socio-cultural impacts. Types of possible positive impacts include :

- Conservation of some traditional cultural patterns because they are attractions for tourists, thus maintaining a sense of cultural heritage and enriching national cultural diversity.
- Improvement of the socio-economic standards of communities through the economic benefits of tourism.
- Encouragement of cross-cultural exchange, both nationally and internationally, through contacts between tourists and residents.

Possible negative socio-cultural impacts include :

- Commercialisation of traditional cultural elements.
- Demonstration effect on the cultures, brought about by tourists, resulting in non-selective imitation by residents of outside cultural traits.
- Disruption of cultural continuity.
- Weakening of cultural identities resulting from the above-described sectors.

The plan makes the point that negative socio-cultural impacts result from many outside influences, not only from tourism.

The plan explains that a socio-cultural programme should be organised and implemented. This programme would focus on conservation of certain selected elements of traditional cultures, and on the controlling of the negative effects of tourism. The sequence of the conservation strategy should be: (1) inventory of traditional cultural elements; (2) selection of the appropriate elements for conservation; and (3) applying conservation measures. The plan indicates that the traditional elements which should, and feasibly can be, conserved and their conservation techniques are :

- *Dance and music*—training at all levels and organisation of performances and contests, including tourist performances.
- *Textile weaving and other handicrafts*—maintenance of quality control, development of a greater variety of crafts, and improvement of production and marketing through village cooperatives and handicraft centres, with sales to tourists.
- *Special cultural events*—organisation of traditional special events and ceremonies on a regular basis, and maintenance of their authenticity.
- *Traditional villages, historic buildings and archaeological sites*—application of conservation measures, including to culturally representative villages.
- *Traditional and historic artefacts*—establishment of museums and organisation of special cultural and historic exhibits.

The plan indicates that establishment of cultural centres can be an important technique for cultural conservation, because they provide suitable physical facilities and can organise cultural programmes.

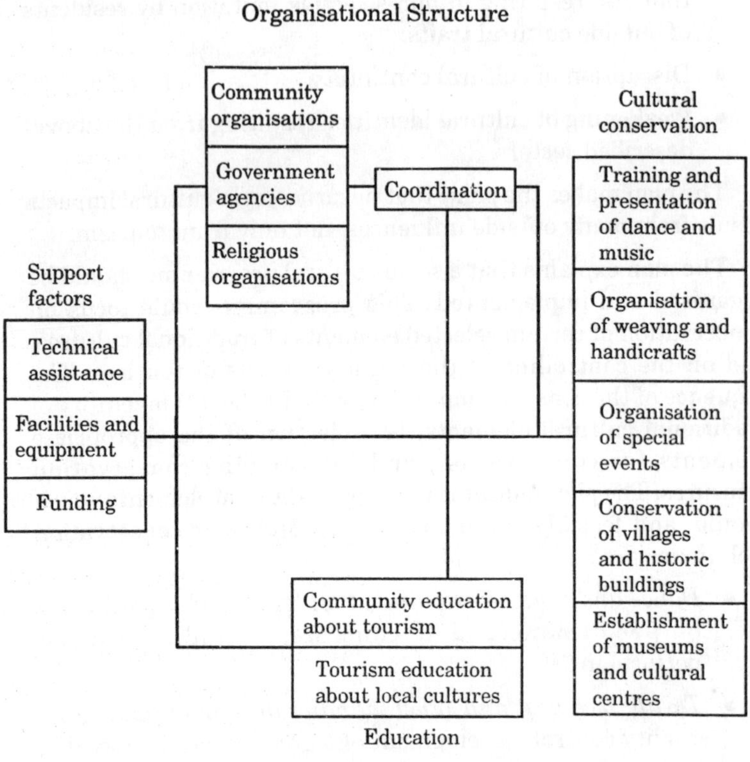

Fig. 18.1 : Socio-cultural programme for Nusa Tenggara.

Based on this approach, the plan sets forth a socio-cultural programme. This is reproduced in Figure 18.1. The various organisations and agencies which should be involved in implementing this programme are specified in the plan.

The plan also recommends that there be community education about all aspects of tourism. This should be carried out in two ways—through formal government channels such as the tourism offices providing information to the media of newspapers, radio and television and to towns and villages in the tourism areas; and through non-government channels of local cultural, youth, religious and community organisations, and traditional leaders. Holding meetings on tourism in towns and villages is recommended as an important communications technique.

The plan emphasises that it is necessary to inform tourists properly about the socio-cultural characteristics of the Nusa Tenggara people before they visit the region and during their tour. In this manner, tourists will have a more meaningful experience and more respect for the local cultures.

Other recommendations of the tourism plan also relate to socio-cultural considerations. The overall policy is for gradual, controlled growth of tourism according to staged and programmed development. Also, no intensive type of tourism development was recommended, except for some low-density beach resorts. Many recommendations are made for conservation of specific archaeological, historic and cultural sites, including certain traditional villages. The importance of incorporating traditional design motifs and local building materials in the development of tourist facilities is stressed.

The plan recommends that there be a follow-through project on village tourism. The concept is that local village develop, own and manage small-scale tourist facilities for visitors who wish to gain a better understanding of the village culture by living there for a while. The facilities, such as simple accommodation and a restaurant, would be built in the local architectural style, and visitors would eat local cuisine and participate in village activities. Some of the villages in the Nusa Tenggara village tourism programme would be organised to serve as base camps for tourists hiking and camping in the nearby mountains. In these villages, in addition to development of accommodation and restaurants, the villages would rent camping equipment and provide guide services.

Conclusions

The socio-cultural element of the Nusa Tenggara tourism plan represents a systematic approach. The local socio-cultural characteristics are surveyed and analysed relative to developing tourism. The possible positive and negative impacts of tourism are identified. Cultural conservation policies and a strategy are set forth, and the traditional elements to be conserved are specified. A recommended socio-cultural programme is presented in diagrammatic form and explained in detail in the plan. Such a specific programmed approach is more likely to be understood and implemented that if merely a list of policy recommendations had been presented.

Important recommendations are to educate residents about tourism and inform tourists about local traditions. It is noteworthy that in both the socio-cultural and education programmes, the plan emphasises that community, religious and traditional organisations and leaders, as well as the government, should be involved. In the case of this region, and many others in the world, these non-government organisations and leaders exercise much influence in their societies. Although not mentioned in the plan, education about tourism could also be included in the curriculum of public and private schools.

More generally, the plan recommends ways to minimise negative impacts and integrate tourism into the society. The gradual, staged approach to developing tourism will give residents time to adapt to it, and learn how to participate in its development and benefits. Conservation of important physical sites, which are attractions for tourists, will also preserve significant symbols of the various societies' cultural heritage. Use of traditional styles in tourist facilities reinforces the local architectural heritage, integrates the buildings into the cultural environment and makes these facilities more acceptable to local residents.

Conserving culturally representative villages and buildings is an important recommendation. In this region, as well as many other places, traditional village buildings are being lost. This is happening, in part, because traditional buildings are now often more expensive to construct and maintain than modern buildings. Also, they typically do not offer the amenities that their occupants want. Therefore, there is a tendency to completely discard traditional styles for modern ones. By deliberately conserving representative examples of traditional villages—including their layouts as well as buildings—residents can appreciate this major aspect of their cultural heritage. They become major attractions for tourists, and tourism helps pay for their conservation. Also an important approach, now being used in some places, is to adapt traditional building styles to modern living, thus evolving a new vernacular architecture in these areas.

The village tourism programme provides the opportunity for tourists to have contact with local residents and participate on a equal basis in their life style. This helps expand cross-cultural understanding. At the same time, it generates direct employment and income to residents and the opportunity for them to develop entrepreneurial skills. However, such programmes must be carefully organised and managed to be successful—with training, advice and often financial assistance made available to the villagers.

19

Incentives in Cyprus Tourism

The investment incentives proposed for Cyprus represent an effective and imaginative approach to encourage the types of tourism projects that reinforce the tourism development strategy of the country. The incentives are specifically tailored to the investment needs of the strategy.

Background

The background of tourism in the Republic of Cyprus and the tourism planning approach and development strategy were presented in a previous case study, and so are only summarized here. Cyprus is an already substantially developed tourist destination based primarily on coastal and beach tourism. Development of tourism has been quite rapid since the mid-1970s, reaching 1.7 million arrivals in 1990. However, concern had been expressed since the early 1980s that there was too much dependency on coastal tourism and that some of the costal tourism areas were beginning to experience environmental problems. If these problems were not remedied and the present trends shifted, they would continue to become worse in the future. However, tourism was also viewed as an important economic sector that would need to expand. The three main objectives of the government on tourism development are to accomplish :

- Growth of tourism's contribution to the Gross Domestic Product.
- Protection of the environmental and cultural qualities of Cyprus.
- Attraction of higher expenditure tourists.

The attraction of higher expenditure tourists would result in increased income from tourism without a corresponding increase in the number of tourist arrivals, thus assisting with environmental and cultural protection.

In order to achieve these objectives, a national tourism development plan was prepared in 1988 (UNDP and WTO, 1988. *Comprehensive Tourism Development Plan for Cyprus.* Madrid: WTO). The planning approach is a comprehensive one that examines all elements of tourism. It includes a detailed environmental analysis and carrying capacity study of the beaches. Market growth targets are established based on the government's economic development objectives, as well as the proposed development strategy. Institutional elements are given careful consideration, and implementation techniques are specified.

The proposed tourism development strategy is that of controlled growth. Within that framework, consolidation of the existing-tourism areas, with new development being located in these areas, is recommended. Consolidation, as opposed to dispersed development, is seen as the best way to provide the resources necessary to carry out environmental quality improvements in these areas. In addition, the plan strongly recommends that a programme of tourism product diversification and improvement be undertaken. This is important in order to attract the desired higher spending international tourists, broaden the tourist markets generally, and better serve domestic tourism needs. Product diversification can also reduce the problem of the seasonality of tourist arrivals that currently prevails.

As part of the institutional considerations for implementation of the overall development strategy, the plan carefully examines the investment incentives needed. In order to understand the investment incentives that are recommended, it is first necessary to review the product improvement strategy.

Product Improvement Strategy

Since the early 1980s, the government has recognised the need for tourism product enrichment. The 1988 tourism plan reinforces this need. It states that, although Cyprus currently has a successful tourism sector, the tourism product is limited compared to that of competing destinations. The accommodation facilities and services are generally good, but only a narrow range of recreational and entertainment facilities are available. Competing destinations are developing accommodation tailored to specific market segments and offering diversified products. They achieve economies of scale through development of larger-scale projects. The plan also notes that the domestic market in Cyprus is changing from its traditional pattern of non-active tourism in the hinterland villages to more active holidays requiring recreational facilities.

The plan emphasises that Cyprus possesses a wide range of both natural and man-made resources that have potential for greater development. There is much opportunity to enrich the tourism product in order to achieve qualitative growth of tourism, for the benefit of both international and domestic tourism. The plan indicates that the strategy for product improvement lies in the following areas :

- Diversification of accommodation and associated facilities aimed toward both existing and new market segments—these can include holiday villages and club-type developments offering a wide range of recreational and leisure facilities.
- Further improvements of archaeological sites, historic buildings and other cultural attractions, utilising imaginative interpretation techniques.
- Greater promotional efforts directed to encouraging use of the mountainous hinterland for overnight stays, sightseeing and other activities, and development of village tourism including village conservation programmes.
- Development of yachting and sailing facilities and related marine tourism environments and golf courses, pending determination of their market and financial feasibility.
- Encouragement of the organisation and promotion of festivals and special events.
- Promotion of opportunities to enjoy a wide range of peripheral activities.
- Encouragement of developments that generate higher tourist expenditure in entertainment, shopping, etc.

The plan elaborates on this product improvement strategy.

Product Development Incentives

The plan examines investment incentives with respect to how these can be used to encourage development of the product improvements needed. The existing incentives are reviewed. The plan determines that they have not been particularly successful in attracting investment in the desired types of product diversification. The main reasons for their lack of success are stated as follows :

- Uncertainty about the likely returns on investment due to its non-accommodation nature.
- Large land area requirements in appropriate locations.
- Lack of local knowledge and experience regarding the type of projects, their planning, organisation and operations.
- Scepticism of banks to support projects with an apparent high degree of risk.

The first point is considered of particular importance. If ancillary facilities, such as golf courses or marinas are not included as part of an accommodation project, they are likely to be less attractive as investments. Consequently, future product improvement schemes should include accommodation alongwith the desired ancillary facilities.

Leading from this analysis, the plan recommends that all government incentives for tourism development not relating to the product improvements needed should be removed. Furthermore, allowances for those projects consistent with the product improvement strategy should be approached as follows :

- Increasing investment allowances for buildings in new products and product improvement schemes.
- Providing accelerated depreciation allowances for capital expenditures incurred for the acquisition of fixed capital assets comprising new plant and construction of buildings in relation to product improvement projects.
- Providing ten-year tax holidays for tourism enterprises undertaking large-scale product improvement projects. The plan states that this overlaps the investment and depreciation allowances but has an important psychological effect and can be especially attractive to foreign investors.

The plan observes that many types of product improvement projects, such as integrated resort hotels, require relatively large land areas. In order to overcome the problems of land assembly and high land costs, the plan recommends that government should consider entering into joint venture arrangements by providing land and infrastructure for key projects. Also, public land could be made available on a selective basis to encourage the desired type of development. This would reduce the private sector investment required, with the government (or local authority) receiving an equity share, based on the value of the land and infrastructure contributed. Eventually, the private company could buy out the government's equity share.

The plan indicates that limited local capital is available for large-scale project. Also there is lack of local experience in developing and managing these projects. Therefore, it recommends that more foreign participation be allowed in the investment and management of those projects which provide product enrichment.

The plan also recommends that the existing Fund for Financing Priority Projects, which has been used for financing some accommodation projects, be more specifically oriented to encouraging tourism product improvements. This should include allowing accommodation financing only when it involves a major ancillary facility such as a golf course, marina or water sports facility. The Fund already allows financing for tourism development in hill resorts, supplementary tourist facilities that provide entertainment, and camping sites. Concurrently, disincentives should be adopted to discourage development of accommodation that is not compatible with the qualitative growth image. These disincentives include high licence fees for developments which do not contribute to product improvements, and other techniques.

Many local investors in Cyprus have only sufficient capital to make investments in small-scale accommodation projects, but these projects typically do not improve the tourism product. The plan recommends ways in which these investors can participate in larger-scale product enrichment projects. Also, the plan indicates that small investors can make a contribution to product improvement by developing high quality and specialised accommodation—such as retreat type marine and mountain resorts and village tourism. The plan suggests that the government set up some pilot projects suitable for small investors.

Conclusions

The plan, as well as the government, recognises that Cyprus must diversify and improve its tourism product. If it does not accomplish this, the country will not be able to continue competing effectively with other tourist destinations, or achieve its objective of attracting higher spending tourists. This represents a progressive approach in that it anticipates possible future problems, even though tourism is currently successful in attracting tourists. The product improvement strategy is very much in keeping with present tourism trends—more tourists now want to be involved in recreation, sports, cultural and other activity and learning experiences; there is increasing market segmentation of tourists including many special interest tourist markets; the older and retired persons tourist markets are rapidly growing with many of these tourists seeking activity-oriented holidays; more tourists are taking shorter but more frequent vacations throughout the year.

The investment incentives recommended for Cyprus reflect the principle that incentives should be specifically designed to achieve the desired type of development—in this case to diversify and improve the tourism product. In the Cyprus plan, incentives are formulated as an integral element of the implementation programme for the proposed development and related product improvement strategy. Consequently, they are more likely to be effective than if they had been prepared in isolation from the strategy.

The approach to formulating the incentives is logical in that it first reviews the present incentives, and determines why they have not been very effective in attracting investment in the desired future types of projects. The approach is comprehensive in that it considers all possible types of incentives. It also considers the need to provide disincentives which will discourage the types of projects that are not compatible with the development strategy.

The plan recognises that part of achieving product diversification is to encourage large-scale projects, such as integrated resorts, that include profit-making accommodation alongwith the less profitable ancillary recreation, sports and entertainment facilities. This presents a dilemma in Cyprus as well as many other island destinations in the world. These places often have similar problems—high land costs and difficulty in assembling large parcels of land; limited capital of local investors who are able to invest only in small-scale profit-making accommodation; and limited local experience in developing and managing large-scale tourism projects. The incentives programme in the plan addresses these issues. It indicates that government and foreign involvement in such projects will be necessary for the long-term benefit of tourism. In order not to discourage local small investments in tourism, which is highly desirable in most places, the plan suggests ways in which small investors can still participate in tourism development.

Although not related to provision of incentives, the government will need to make some direct investments in improving the tourism product. For example, archaeological and historic sites require improved interpretation, and additional cultural and public-type recreation facilities need to be developed. Admission fees can cover some of the cost of this type of investment. In any case, the increased overall benefits from tourism, including government revenues from this sector, usually justify the public investment required.

20

Manpower Planning and Training in the Oman Tourism

The manpower planning and training component of the Oman tourism plan represents the recognised approach to providing the trained personnel required for proper management and operation of the tourism sector. At the same time, it takes into account the particular constraints that exist in Oman.

Background

The background of Oman and the tourism planning approach used there were presented in a previous case study, and so are only summarized here. Located in the southeastern corner of the Arabian Peninsula, the Sultanate of Oman offers a diversity of tourist attractions. Natural features include scenic beauty, beaches and other interesting environmental features. Cultural attractions relate to the long history of the country—the traditions of historic towns and villages; and numerous archaeological and historic monuments. During recent years, the production and export of oil has provided the country with the means for achieving rapid economic development.

Although business travel is well developed in the country, holiday tourism is new. International holiday tourists have been allowed into the country only since 1987, and still comprise a small proportion of total tourist arrivals. Now the country wishes to diversify the economy and develop tourism in a very carefully controlled manner. Tourism is to be developed based only on the inherent natural and cultural/historic features of the country, and not be aimed at attracting the 'mass' tourist markets.

Protection of the environment and culture is of utmost concern in developing tourism.

The national tourism plan for Oman was prepared in 1991 (UNDP and WTO, 1991. *National Plan for Tourism—Sultanate of Oman*. Madrid: WTO). The planning approach is a comprehensive one, with emphasis on controlled development. Both international and domestic tourism are considered. The tourism development concept is based on providing opportunities for informed tourists to experience the special cultural and environmental features of Oman. Six tourism zones are designated—three primary zones of attractions and three secondary zones. The major types of attractions are indicated for each zone. The plan also identifies several special interest themes based on flora, fauna and the country's history. The plan recommends various tourist itineraries, circuits and excursions. A marketing strategy is proposed which emphasises image-building and selective promotion.

Implementation of the plan considers several elements relating to organisational structures, procedural controls, promotional measures, planning actions required, and detailed planning of certain priority projects and areas. An important element of the implementation programme is manpower planning and training.

A particular characteristic of manpower planning for tourism in Oman is the relatively poor cultural, religious and social image of the hotel and catering industry as an employer. There is not a tradition in the country of working in many of the activities associated with tourism, and especially in food and beverage service. Additionally, it is difficult to attract Omanis to work in the private sector generally for various reasons, including the greater appeal of working for government agencies. However, the present government policy is for Omanisation of the work force including in tourism, and decreasing the country's dependence on foreign workers. Other manpower planning considerations are that Omani women traditionally do not work outside their homes, although this is changing rapidly. Finally, with its small population and rapid economic development, there tends not to be a great oversupply of local labour available in Oman, especially in the urban areas.

Manpower Supply and Demand

The planning team reviewed an existing national study of labour supply and demand for the entire economy of Oman, prepared by the World Bank in 1985. That study revealed that there is a much higher proportion of males than females in the education system as a whole, but there is a more balanced distribution of students taking business and commercial courses. The World Bank study projected the number of persons completing various education levels and entering the work force from 1985 to 1995. This provided the tourism study team with a general basis for determining the availability of persons to work in tourism at various skill, supervisory and management levels.

As the first step of the manpower planning analysis of the tourism plan, a survey was conducted of existing employment in hotels. Based on this survey and the projected accommodation needs in the plan, manpower needs are projected to 1995, 2000 and 2005. The projection figures are based on employee/bed ratios and include accommodation for business as well as holiday tourists. This projection is distributed by occupation and education/skills level categories as follows :

- *General management*—graduate, diploma/certificate and advanced skills levels.
- *Specialist management*—graduate, diploma/certificate and advanced skills levels.
- *Food preparation and kitchen*—advanced skills, skilled and low skills levels.
- *Food and beverage service*—advanced skills, skilled and low skills levels.
- *Reception/telephone/administration/clerical*—advanced skills, skilled and low skills levels.
- *Housekeeping*—advanced skills, skilled and low skills levels.
- *Other*—advanced skills, skilled and low skills levels.

For each of these categories, separate projections are made for Omani and expatriate workers. Total employment needs are projected to more than double from the present level, reaching almost 6,000 persons in 2005. A much greater proportion of Omanis are projected to work in hotels in the future, based on the recommended training and other programmes being carried out. The manpower needs for tour and travel operations, including tour guides, and tourism management in the government are also examined.

Manpower Training

The plan reviews the present status of training of tourism employees. It identifies that there is no existing tourism training programme or institute, although such a programme had been proposed in the past. However, some training of hotel employees is carried out by the larger hotels within their own enterprises. The hotels also, of course, employ expatriates who may have had training elsewhere. There has been some overseas training of local tour guides and tourism management officials. Most of the tour and travel operations and management personnel are foreigners who have received their training elsewhere.

Various types of training needs are identified in the plan. The major need is for full-time vocational programmes designed to facilitate entry of Omanis to employment in hotels and other tourism enterprises. Another need is for part-time programmes to improve the skills of persons already working in tourism. This includes upgrading type training of supervisory and management level staff and advanced craft level training of technical staff. The plan indicates that education and training should be regarded as a continuous process throughout a person's life. The training needs of the government tourism office staff in tourism management are also reviewed. The plan recommends that these needs be met through sending the tourism officials outside the country for overseas university programmes and on-the-job attachments. The plan identifies the need for short-term training of tourism-related employees such as drivers of tourism vehicles.

The plan emphasises the importance of English language training in all the programmes. It states that Omanis must be provided with the means to communicate effectively in an industry where English is the language medium. Otherwise, employers will continue to discriminate in favour of expatriates with fluency in English.

The plan proposes that an autonomous tourism training institute be established. This institute should be under the Directorate of Tourism, and funded by the government in partnership with the leading industry enterprises. The institute would initially require some international assistance, including international instructors who would work with and educate Omani counterpart teachers.

The plan states that the institute should have primary responsibility for training of Omanis in full-time programmes, and secondary responsibility for offering part-time and upgrading courses for existing industry employees. The full-time programme should include several specialisations—food and beverage service; food production; housekeeping and reception at the operations and management levels; hotel management; tour guiding; and transportation ticketing. These subjects would be phased in over a period of time. The continuing training programme would include short courses in various specialisations. Omanisation of the tourism work force would be emphasised in the training programmes. A target is set of 500 Omanis trained by 1995. After that time, many more Omanis would be trained, to reach the target of 55 per cent Omanisation of all tourism employees by 2005.

The plan calculates the cost of establishing the institute. It proposes that the existing industry employment levy be allocated to pay for allowances of students, salaries of Omani counterpart teachers and for the cost of the part-time training of industry employees.

The plan examines the factors relative to achieving greater Omanisation of the tourism work force. It points out that, in addition to some reluctance of Omanis to work in tourism for cultural and other reasons, the private hotels prefer employing expatriates because they can be attracted for lower wages than Omanis will accept. However, the government-owned hotels by policy successfully employ Omanis. The plan notes that establishment of the training institute will give a greater sense of status to tourism as a desirable career to follow. Several approaches are proposed in the plan to induce Omanis to select tourism as a career and, at the same time, encourage the private hotels to offer more jobs to Omanis. These include various government initiatives, as follows :

- Undertaking a public awareness programme to educate the general population about the benefits of tourism as an economic activity and as a career.

- Providing proper training of Omanis in tourism skills and English language, with structured periods of industry exposure as part of the training.
- Developing standards of compensation and work conditions that compare favourably with government posts.
- Requiring that hoteliers employ and train Omani staff, but giving them the right to select candidates and to discharge them on reasonable grounds.
- Giving preference to hotels which encourage Omanisation in allocating the sizable amount of government use of accommodation.

The plan emphasises that Omanisation efforts should also include attracting women to tourism employment. It points out that Omani female employees have a high reputation for productivity and punctuality. In effecting Omanisation, the plan notes that the present expatriate employees should be assured that this policy will not threaten their jobs. There will still be need for expatriate employment for many years.

Conclusions

The type of analysis applied in the manpower planning and training component of the Oman tourism plan represents the logical approach to this subject. First the existing employment in tourism is surveyed and any particular problems and needs are noted. Then future manpower needs are projected based on the level of tourism targeted in the tourism plan. Employee/bed ratios are applied in making this projection. Next, the overall human resources available in the country are evaluated, including consideration of expected future education levels of the labour supply—this study had already been completed in Oman. Finally, the training needs are identified and the education and training programmes and recommendations are formulated based on these needs.

The approach used in the plan is comprehensive in that all the types of tourism employment and tourism education and training needs are considered—hotel and catering operations and management; tourism management; tour and travel operations; and employment in related tourist activities.

The major recommendation of the plan is to establish a tourism training institute. Such a specialised training institution is usually required to be established in countries or large regions developing tourism. In places with more limited tourism, a tourism training programme can sometimes be incorporated into an existing vocational school. The Oman plan provides some specification of the proposed institute's programme and a general cost estimate. This can form the basis for preparing the more detailed study of the institute that will be required before it can be developed. The plan justifiably indicates that the institute will require international technical assistance.

A specific consideration underlying this manpower and training study is government's policy for Omanisation of the industrial labour force. For socio-cultural and economic reasons, this policy presents particular challenges in the tourism sector. Similar constraints have faced some other countries where there is traditional reluctance of the local population to work in tourism, and to consider it as a desirable career. The plan systematically examines this situation in Oman in order to understand thoroughly the obstacles to Omanisation. Then it recommends suitable approaches which can be applied to overcome the obstacles and achieve gradual Omanisation.

21

Promotion Strategy and Programme in Uganda Tourism

The promotion strategy and programme for Uganda reflect a realistic approach to commencing the promotion of a country which currently has limited facilities and a weak image but excellent tourist attractions.

Background

The background of Uganda and the tourism planning approach used there were described in a previous case study, and so are only summarised here. Uganda is located in east-central Africa, inland from Kenya. The population of the country is somewhat over 17 million and includes several cultural groups. The capital city of Kampala has about half a million inhabitants. The primary attractions for tourists are outstanding scenic areas, including lakes, rivers, mountains, rainforests and savanna, and a variety of wildlife. Important specific features include Murchison Falls, the Ruwenzori Mountains and mountain gorilla reserves. Ten national parks have been designated although most of these still have limited tourist facilities.

Tourism was relatively well developed in Uganda in the late 1960s and early 1970s. Then, because of political turmoil and changes in government policy, tourism became virtually non-existent. Much of the tourist facility and infrastructure development was damaged or deteriorated through lack of maintenance, and wildlife was decimated. Since the mid-1980s, rehabilitation of the economy has been taking place including of tourism development. Major conservation programmes are being implemented to rejuvenate the wildlife. Substantial progress has been made on rehabilitation, and game populations are recovering, but these programmes are still underway.

The government policy is now for revitalisation of the tourism sector as an important source of economic development. Tourism is also seen as a means to achieve conservation objectives. In 1991, Uganda received 68,000 international tourist arrivals. Only about 10,000 of these arrivals were holiday tourists, with the remainder coming for business, official mission and other purposes. Most of the holiday arrivals were budget types of tourists. The large international and community in Uganda provides many of the present visitors to the national parks.

In the early 1990s, a tourism plan was prepared for Uganda (UNDP and WTO, 1993. *Integrated Tourism Master Plan—Republic of Uganda. Vols. I, II and III.* Madrid: WTO). The planning approach is comprehensive, and examines all aspects of tourism. The development strategy emphasises that tourist market development must take place slowly because tourist facilities and the wildlife will remain rather limited for the next few years. The spatial development concept is based on establishment of tourism zones—three primary, two secondary and three tertiary zones. Several possible tourist circuits are identified which link the tourism zones. The plan recommends that tourist service centres be developed to provide tourist information, nature interpretation exhibits, tourism services, medical clinics and commercial facilities.

Promotion Strategy

The Uganda plan includes a major element in the implementation section on the promotion policy and programme. The national structure plan sets forth the overall marketing and product strategy. It identifies the market target segments, and the product development priorities. The overall target for international holiday tourists is set at a modest level of about 33,000 by 1997. In addition, there will be a sizable number of business type tourists. The holiday tourist market countries are identified as follows—

- Priority A—UK, Germany and USA.
- Priority B—France and Italy.
- Priority C—Australia, rest of Europe, other countries in Africa and Asia.

The promotion strategy notes the progress that is being made in expanding international airline services, hotel development, revival of wildlife resources and improving inbound tour operating services. It indicates that Uganda can be perceived as a newly emerging destination. The plan states that promotion has to tackle three critical problems :

- Image problem that most tourists and even the travel trade believe that Uganda is out of the tourism picture.
- Chronic shortage of any up-to-date informational or promotional material.
- Lack of confidence of the international travel trade that the country has a definite programme for, and commitment to, tourism development.

To overcome these problems, the promotion strategy to 1997 is composed of three elements :

- Project a new image for Uganda, mainly by means of public relations activities with the media and travel trade.
- Make information available to existing and potential tourists, so that present tourists have a more enjoyable visit and offer better world-of-mouth recommendations about the country, and so that potential tourists are informed about what Uganda has to offer and are induced to visit.
- Mount systematic public relations and sales promotion activities, that present what Uganda is doing about developing tourism and generate sales leads for the private sector operators.

The strategy is established for three distinct time phases :

- *1993–94*—initial period during which the present Tourism Department (or its promotion functions) of the Ministry is transformed into a separate autonomous board.
- *1995–97*—full operation of the board with provision of an adequate budget, and implementation of promotional activities.
- *Post–1997*—designing and implementing a more aggressive promotion strategy and programme based on an improved and expanded tourism product, including improved infrastructure.

The plan examines market positioning and product differentiation. It states that Uganda needs to position itself as a new destination, now rebuilding itself, which offers outstanding scenic attractions and exceptional wildlife and rainforests. Other advantages are that the country is English-speaking and a gateway to Zaire and Rwanda. The plan indicates that Uganda will be a 'niche' market for several years and needs to stress its product differentiation from competing or complementary destinations. The country should differentiate its product from that of the Eastern and Southern African plains—which are a different type of environment then that of most of Uganda—and stress the country's rainforests and mountains. The plan identifies several possibilities for combination tours with other countries in the Eastern and Southern African regions, with Uganda offering a somewhat contrasting, but complementary, tourism product.

In terms of tourism image, the plan explains that Uganda should project itself as a country of spectacular scenic beauty that includes interesting wildlife. It should also stress that it is rebuilding itself. The imagery to be projected should be inspirational and emphasise that Uganda is an uncrowded destination which possesses an element of remoteness and adventure. The focus should be on exotic places—Murchison Falls Park with its launch trip up the Nile to the falls; rainforests with mountain gorillas and eco-tourism; and the Ruwenzori Mountains for trekking and mountaineering. This imagery should be projected through use of imaginative photography showing tourist activities related to these attractions, and emphasise that good accommodation and medical centres are available.

The plan recommends a promotional mix, but shifting from the present market of backpackers, truckers and adventurous independent travellers toward a mix of more affluent tourist. These include independent holiday travellers, inclusive tours for adventurers, inclusive 'mainstream' sightseeing tours, trekkers, conservation-oriented and special interest tourists, and regional (African and expatriate) travellers. The recommended promotion techniques are tailored for each type of market.

The plan also recommends an organisational structure to be responsible for promotion. It points out the deficiencies of the present system and lists six conditions necessary to carry out effective promotion :

- Establish a separate promotional entity, such as the already proposed Uganda Tourist Board, able to receive and disburse funds independently of the Treasury.
- House this board separately from the Ministry.
- Provide the board with its own properly maintained equipment.
- Pay adequate wages to the staff, so that they do not need to take second jobs.
- Provide technical assistance to the board.
- Provide a budget (from the government) to the board.

Recommendations are made on the office space and equipment which the board should have. The board could be organised, under a set of directors, into the departments of public relations, sales promotion and administration. Tourist information would be under the public relations department.

Various types of informational and promotional printed materials are recommended. They include guide leaflets, fact sheets, maps, promotional leaflets and a shell folder. Distribution of printed material should be at tourist information points, through direct mail and at exhibitions.

The plan specifies the several functions of the public relations department. It points out that public relations can be much more cost-effective and have longer-term impact than advertising. The opportunities for press coverage are identified. These include coverage of new hotel openings and wildlife conservation activities.

The plan emphasises that use of mailing lists and direct mail promotion are particularly suitable for Uganda because it is initially aiming for niche markets. Direct mail would reach groups which are especially responsive to the appeals of the country. However, other techniques should also be applied. The plan recommends that Uganda features go into brochures of tour operators in the various market countries. Additionally, Uganda should participate in the major tourism trade fairs such as the WTM in London, ITB in Berlin and Travel Trade Fair in Brussels. A modest level of media advertising is suggested including in regional expatriate magazines, for example in Kenya, and specialist travel trade and special interest magazines.

The plan examines the various approaches to budgeting promotional activities. It indicates that a fixed rate ratio based on a percentage of the projected tourist spending provides a guideline for budgeting. A specific promotion and budget programme is set forth, by year from 1993 to 1997. In this programme, most of the first two years are devoted to organising the separate promotion board. The recommended annual budget for promotion would represent about US $ 7 per holiday tourist in 1997. The plan states that this is not an unreasonable figure. In addition to attracting more tourist, it will also help open up new spending opportunities to tourists (by providing them with more information) and shift Uganda toward higher spending tourist markets. The plan notes that the private sector also provides valuable promotion, but that it is directed to promoting individual enterprises.

Conclusions

The promotion strategy and programme for Uganda are logically formulated. The formulation starts with the market targets and product development priorities, examines the current situation, identifies the problems to be tackled, determines a strategy in terms of approaches and time phasing, and sets forth a realistic promotion programme. The market targets are set at a modest level, within the framework of the realities of developing the tourism product, but they still represent a considerable increase over the present level of arrivals. The strategy recognises the importance of creating a tourism image of the country as an essential basis for developing tourism in Uganda, as it is for any newly developing destination. It also recognises that considerable public relations efforts are required to project a desirable image.

The image to be projected—that of exotic scenic beauty and wildlife with a sense of adventure travel—is an imaginative one. It reflects what is unusual about the country, and attempts to differentiate it from the better known Eastern and Southern African countries. It also will prepare the tourists not to expect highly developed facilities and tourism infrastructure. The approach that part of the image focus on the rebuilding of the country should help raise the interest and confidence of tourists to visit Uganda. The initial emphasis on niche markets, but higher spending ones than those who now visit the country, reflects a realistic approach. These markets will make use of the existing limited facilities and get tourism started in the right direction. Many of the niche markets, such as eco- and special interest tourism, will likely remain as important markets in the future even after more general interest tourism has been developed.

The strategy rightfully recognises the essential need to establish an autonomous and properly organised, staffed, equipped and funded promotion board. This is a basic organisational ingredient in carrying out successful marketing in almost any country. Because of their importance, the public relations functions of this board are specified in detail.

The promotional mix of techniques to be utilised are those which meet the specific requirements of image-building and attracting the desired types of tourists. Many of the niche markets, for example, can best be tapped through direct mailing of information. The types of informational and promotional materials are specified. They are kept to a realistic level within the budgetary and technical capabilities to product. The promotional budget that is recommended reflects what is required to undertake effective marketing, without being extravagant.

The promotional approach applied in the Uganda tourism plan is a comprehensive one. In addition to the considerations referred to in the plan, however, the country will also need to decide whether to establish overseas offices, an expensive type of operation, or some other form of overseas representation. Also a consideration is to what extent can the public and private sectors cooperate on joint promotion programmes, including joint funding of promotion, aimed at image-building and general marketing.

22

Promotion Programme in Sri Lanka Tourism

The marketing strategy and promotion programme of Sri Lanka are specific and comprehensive. They particularly reflect the close relationship that must be maintained between product development and marketing.

Background

Sri Lanka is located off the southeastern tip of India. The country's geography is varied. Central highlands of mountains and high plains are flanked by coastal flat and hilly lowlands. The climate is tropical with distinct dry and wet zones and seasonal distribution of rainfall. The southwest monsoon, which occurs between May and September, mainly affects the southwestern part of the country. The northeast monsoon, which takes place between November and February, affects the eastern areas. This results in the east and west coasts of the island having complementary tourist seasons.

Sri Lanka's population is estimated to be 17.2 million, of which more than 600,000 live in the main city and commercial centre of Colombo on the west coast. The majority of people live in villages and rural areas. Some 74 per cent of the population is Sinhalese, 19 per cent Tamil, and the remainder composed of various other groups. About 70 per cent of the population is Buddhist and 15 per cent is Hindu. The country has a long, interesting and varied history. There has been much indigenous cultural development, as well as many outside influences from India and various European colonial powers.

Sri Lanka possesses a great diversity of attractions for tourists. Natural features inc le many beaches and related marine areas, scenic beauty, abundant flora and wildlife, waterfalls and thermal springs. The country has 11 national parks, a marine sanctuary, and several nature and forest reserves. Archaeological and historic features include some major sites. Five of these places, termed the ancient cities', are located in the central part of the country. The comprise what is called the Cultural Triangle of Sri Lanka. These five places, another historic monument and an ecologically important rainforest have been designated by UNESCO as World Heritage Sites. There are several other significant attraction features—ancient irrigation works; tea plantations and processing plants; gem mines; botanical gardens; spice gardens; an elephant orphanage; traditional dance and music; major religious festivals; a wide range of handicrafts; and convention facilities in Colombo.

International tourism in Sri Lanka commenced in the 1960s and grew rapidly until the early 1980s. In 1968, a tourism plan was prepared for the country and partially implemented, particularly the development of an integrated resort on the southwest coast. From 1983, tourism suffered a major decline as a result of civil unrest within the country. Tourism operations greatly decreased and hotel occupancies and profitability were severely eroded. Proposed new investments were abandoned and only the most essential maintenance of facilities was carried out.

Tourism has recovered remarkably since 1990. There were almost 320,000 international tourist arrivals in 1991. With the resurgence of tourism, many hotels have been rehabilitated. By 1993, however, there had not been sufficient time for all the products to be brought up to full standard.

The access for virtually all international tourists to Sri Lanka is by air to the airport near Colombo. Most tourism development is based on beach-oriented accommodation on the west coast. There is some limited accommodation situated inland. However, many tourists staying in the coastal areas take tours to the Cultural Triangle, national parks, tea plantations and other places. Colombo has several high quality urban hotels.

Tourism Planning Approach

In the early 1990s, a new tourism plan for Sri Lanka was prepared (UNDP and WTO, 1992. *Sri Lanka Tourism Master*

Plan. Madrid: WTO). This plan is quite detailed and examines all aspects of tourism. It focuses on review of the current situation, a long-term strategic plan for 2001, a five-year development programme and pre-feasibility studies for selected priority projects. Both international and domestic tourism are considered in the plan. The planning analysis indicates that the country has considerable scope to expand its tourism industry, while still maintaining sustainable development. It states that Sri Lanka possesses major tourism resources which can be developed into a richer and more varied tourism product range attracting a broad spectrum of tourist markets.

The recommended strategy for tourism development is four-fold—diversify the market mix; increase tourist spending by developing and upgrading tourist facilities; increase the emphasis on cultural, natural and other tourist attractions; and create a positive image for Sri Lanka. The plan indicates that through this strategy, the economic benefits of tourism can be maximised, while environmental degradation and social problems will be minimised. The strategy calls for a carefully planned approach to developing tourism.

An optimum market target of 874,000 international tourist arrivals is established for 2001. A doubling in real terms of the average daily tourist expenditure is projected from 1991 to 2001. This increase of arrivals and expenditures will require a doubling of the present number of accommodation rooms. Emphasis will be on development of high and medium quality hotels. Foreign exchange receipts are projected to increase greatly by 2001. Some 70 per cent of these receipts will be retained in the country. Employment in tourism will also substantially increase.

The development strategy identifies 14 tourism zones throughout the country. Within these zones, the major product development proposals are as follows :

- New planned and integrated developments providing a range of facilities and services, catering to different international and domestic tourist markets and day visitors.
- Rehabilitation and upgrading of existing tourism areas in a comprehensive and coordinated way.

- Provision of a diversity of tourist attractions, including the major cultural, historic and wildlife attractions and related small-scale tourism development.
- Development of domestic tourist facilities, where they are not already covered in the other categories.
- Organisation of new tour routes alongwith improvement of existing routes.

Two key elements of the strategy are encouraging planned developments in designated places and the opening up of new tourism areas. The plan strongly recommends that development incentives for the private sector be retained and extended to cover upgrading of existing facilities. Recommendations are made on several other elements—international air transportation; other transportation; economic enhancement; manpower training; organisation and coordination; social aspects; community tourism; cultural heritage; environmental protection; and development guidelines. The plan states that implementation should be given priority, with establishment of a high level committee to oversee implementation.

Marketing Strategy

The plan first examines the factors that determine the marketing strategy—the civil unrest that prevailed during most of the 1980s; the wide and not always accurate international media coverage of this unrest; the lack of awareness in source markets of the extensive range of attractions available the seasonality of tourism, variable accommodation standards; the need to improve quality; the importance of achieving sustainable tourism; and the social effects of tourism.

Marketing objectives are set forth in the plan, as follows :

- Develop the perception in the major source market countries of Sri Lanka as a destination offering quality attractions; facilities and experiences.
- Design and execute marketing activities which build on Sri Lanka's distinctive features and advantages.
- Attract additional high spending tourists, taking account of various ways in which spending can be enhanced.

- Create destination awareness by the government, which facilitates the private sector in its own marketing efforts.
- Develop and penetrate further the traditional markets of Western Europe.
- Expand penetration in the regional Asian markets, particularly Japan, South Korea and India, as well as in Australia, North America and the Middle East.
- Conduct marketing and promotional activities targeted at market segments identified by ongoing market research.
- Promote the full range of tourist attractions and facilities developed throughout Sri Lanka.
- Achieve a more balanced distribution of tourist flows within the country in line with the development area strategy.
- Undertake seasonal and other types of promotion to improve the utilisation of tourist operations to a profitable year-round level.

Based on these objectives, a three-point marketing strategy is recommended:

- Build up in the major tourist generating markets the perceptions of Sri Lanka as a destination offering a diverse range of quality attractions, facilities and experiences. All of these are readily accessible and exist in a vibrant and relaxing environment, without threat to personal safety.
- Differentiate Sri Lanka in terms of its tourist attractions, facilities and services from its neighbours, in particular India and the Maldives.
- Stress the high degree of emphasis being given to ensuring that the scale, pace and type of Sri Lanka's tourism development is sustainable, with respect to both the society and culture of the people and the country's outstanding natural resources.

The strategy elaborates on the specific attractions and other product improvements which should be undertaken to achieve a diversity of quality tourists attractions, facilities and experiences.

For domestic tourism, the plan specifies three promotion objectives—encourage travel for religious, cultural and recreational purposes among all parts of the community; promote youth travel; and encourage at least one annual holiday to be taken by employed people. The proposed strategy for promoting domestic tourism is set forth, as follows :

- Formulate and promote a 'Discover Sri Lanka' campaign.
- Promote one-week or weekend-inclusive packages.
- Promote holiday-taking through seminars and exhibits at various places.
- Publicise domestic tourism through newspaper holiday supplements and editorial coverage.
- Enlist the cooperation of the industry, trade unions and service organisations to develop and promote domestic tourism.
- Develop holiday guides for distribution.
- Evaluate the possibility of promoting the formulation and introduction of holiday schemes similar to those operated by *Comités d'Enterprise* (Works Councils) in France.

Promotion Programme

Based on the marketing objectives and strategy, the plan recommends a specific promotion programme. This is related to the target markets according to the time table of the first five years of the plan. In determining the promotion programme, the plan first identifies the deficiencies related to present promotion activities. Among these are insufficient marketing staff and funding and the need for more market research. The plan recommends that consumer surveys in the five major market countries be undertaken in the immediate future.

On market positioning, the plan points out that the present image of Sri Lanka needs to be more focused on a single recognisable theme. On organisation for marketing, the plan indicates that the respective roles of the government and private sector be clearly defined, with their promotional activities closely coordinated. Recommendations are made on the best approach to overseas representation—establishing overseas offices in the major market countries, contracting representation companies for other market countries, and making some use of individual representation and public relations agencies. The primary, secondary and opportunity market countries are identified.

Priorities are set forth for the specific market segments to promote during the short-, medium- and long-term periods.

The plan describes the promotion techniques that should be used for the travel trade and potential tourists in the primary, secondary and opportunity markets. It emphasises that because of its limited marketing budget, Sri Lanka should carefully direct its marketing efforts at well-defined targets, using the most effective techniques. Each type of promotion technique and activity is described and related to the relevant target markets.

A detailed promotion programme is recommended, and the estimated costs are specified. The plan points out that the total promotion budget, expressed as a percentage of gross tourism earnings, is within the range of similar budgets of many competing destinations—3-5 per cent. A calculation is presented of the proposed marketing expenditure per target tourist arrival in the various market countries. Sources of funding for the promotion programme are proposed. The plan strongly emphasises that a fully coordinated and collaborative approach to marketing is necessary. It recommends that the Tourism Marketing Committee, which has already been proposed, the organised in the near future.

Conclusions

Sri Lanka is an example of a country that has a great diversity of outstanding natural and cultural tourist attractions. However, it has in the past relied mostly on beach-oriented tourism and, in large part, attracted lower spending tourist markets. The development of tourism and the image of the country as a tourist destination do not reflect the tourism resources that are available. Compounding the image problem is the recent civil unrest which has been highly publicised in the international media. The development strategy is focused on improving and greatly expanding the tourism product of attractions, facilities and experiences. This will provide the basis for steady but substantial growth of tourism that has better balanced development throughout the country.

The marketing strategy for international tourism is derived directly from the development strategy and the need to project a focused and positive image. It is logically formulated based on identification of marketing problems and the marketing objectives. A key principle applied in formulating the marketing strategy is maintaining its close relationship to the development strategy, which emphasises product improvements and diversification. The strategy approach also examines organisational and funding problems which need to be resolved in order to effectively implement marketing.

The marketing strategy for domestic tourism is interesting in that it considers the need to expose Sri Lankans to the concept of taking local holidays. This is a new type of activity for many residents of the country. The strategy also suggests ways in which holiday-taking can be made more feasible for Sri Lankans.

The promotion programme examines all the possible techniques of promotion. It justifiably recommends that the techniques applied be closely related to specific target markets, as the most efficient use of promotional resources. Overseas representation is always a major consideration in marketing because of the high cost involved. The Sri Lanka programme carefully examines the best approach to overseas representation. A fundamentally important type of recommendation made is the definition of the respective roles in marketing between the public and private sectors. Without this definition of respective roles and responsibilities, there can be contradictory images of the country projected and duplication of promotional efforts.

The promotion programme emphasises the importance of maintaining close coordination between the public and private sectors on promotional activities. This type of coordination is needed in many countries. Finally, the programme makes a strong case for adequately funding promotion, as an essential element in achieving successful expansion of tourism.

23

Standards in Philippines Tourism

The tourism plan for the Philippines contains standards and guidelines for developing tourist facilities. These reflect a sound environmental approach to integrating facilities into their natural and man-made setting whilst, at the same time, fulfilling their functional purposes.

Background

The background of the tourism development plan for the Philippines was described in a previous case study, and so is only summarised here. As a large multi-island country with various ethnic groups, the Philippines offer a diversity of natural and cultural attractions and activities for tourists. There has already been considerable development of tourism in the country, but tourism is experiencing some problems. Tourism is overly concentrated in the capital city region of Manila with limited development elsewhere in the country. Thus, economic benefits from tourism are not well distributed throughout the country. Also the flow of tourist arrivals is erratic because of the influences of natural disasters and political events. The country has considerable potential to expand tourism, for this sector to make a greater contribution to the country's economy and society.

The tourism planning approach is a comprehensive one that examines and makes recommendations on all aspects of tourism (UNDP and WTO, 1991. *Tourism Master Plan for the Republic of the Philippines*. Madrid: WTO). The planning study is organised based on formulating a long-range plan, medium-term development programme, and detailed plans for priority destination areas. Time periods are established for recommending development objectives, strategies and policies, up to the plan's horizon year of 2010. The overall strategy is based on the concept of decentralisation by developing three tourism clusters or regions, each focused on a major international gateway. Within each region are satellite tourism areas, many of which would be integrated resorts. From a marketing and product development standpoint, tourism would be based on a combination of a general interest 'mass' market and special interest 'niche' markets.

The development standards and guidelines in the plan are organised according to site planning, environmental protection, building development and utilities. These were prepared particularly for the several tourism areas for which detailed plans were formulated.

Site Planning Considerations

With respect to site planning considerations, the plan makes several recommendations. In coastal locations, the common use facilities, such as swimming pools and restaurants, are best located close to and facing the beach, but still maintaining the required minimum setbacks from the beach. Accommodation facilities, however, are often best situated on promontories or hills, further from the beach but offering good views. Service facilities, such as parking and utility areas, should be in convenient locations but not be obtrusive or block views.

The plan indicates that careful land clearing and grading should be done, making sure that special environmental features such as hills and other natural landforms are preserved and enhanced. Large trees and other important vegetation should not be removed or disturbed. In coastal sites, the beach area should be cleared of litter. Swimming areas may be improved with clearing of rocks, dead coral and other material, but only with strict controls applied so that marine disturbance is minimised.

Ten-metre buffer zones, where no development is allowed, are recommended along the entire perimeter of tourist facility area including golf courses. These buffer zones should be mounded and landscaped.

The plan emphasises that the coastline should be left undeveloped, in order to allow for natural coastal ecological processes to continue. A mandatory beach-front zone of 30 metres inland from the beach vegetation line should be maintained in its natural condition, except for careful landscaping. Any buildings and other structures should be set back 30 metres from the vegetation line. There may be exceptions made to this setback requirement in special circumstances, but only if an environmental impact assessment has been prepared. Piers, groins and breakwaters must be designed based on a detailed study of beach, water and underwater characteristics.

Various building setbacks are recommended. Buildings should be set back 5 metres from the edge of green areas. The recommended minimum distances between buildings vary from 7 to 10 metres, depending on the types of buildings.

The plan recommends that landscaping plans must be prepared for development sites. Landscaping should give preference to large shade trees along roads and footpaths, coconut and other palm trees along the beach-front, and flowering bushes and other pants in various places. 'Colour' landscaping can be achieved by the coordinated planting of flowering trees and bushes that bloom at different times of the year. Landscaping should consider not only beautification and enhancement of the natural character of the resort, but also the need to provide privacy, absorb noise and serve as wind barriers. Existing vegetation should be preserved as much as possible.

The plan recommends density requirements based on the concept of gross density—the maximum number of rooms allowed within a given hotel or resort site. The density recommendations are as follows :

- *High density*—60–80 rooms per hectare
- *Medium density*—30–45 rooms per hectare
- *Low density*—10–15 rooms per hectare

The plan indicates that parking areas should be designed in a landscaped cluster manner including landscaping around the areas. Other parking design guidelines are recommended. All facilities, grounds, beach areas and the tourism zones generally should be well maintained.

For implementation of site planning standards, the plan recommends that preparation of a site development plan be required for each hotel or resort site. These plans must be submitted to the local development authority for review, evaluation and approval. Also, an environmental impact assessment must be conducted by a competent body for each proposed development before a construction permit can be issued.

Environmental Protection

The plan gives particular attention to protection of the marine habitat. It notes that there has already been serious damage of this habitat in many places. The plan recommends that the coral reef, seagrass bed and mangrove areas should be assessed and zoned for appropriate uses. Strict protection measures should be applied to the undamaged marine areas so that they can properly serve their important ecological functions.

The plan makes specific recommendations for marine habitat conservation. The commercial sale of corals, shells and mangrove wood should be prohibited as should the manufacture of decorations from corals, shells and other marine products. The disposal of garbage at sea by boats and any other sea-going craft should be prohibited.

The plan points out that a serious threat to the marine environment in the country is dynamite fishing. This activity has destroyed or damaged many coral reefs. Dynamiting must be stopped; but the problem is that fishermen make their livelihood from this type of fishing. The plan indicates that an alternative source of income should be developed for the fishermen. It suggests a cooperative fishing approach that utilises fish traps, which has been successfully developed in some places. Associated with the fish traps, fish storage cages could be installed in the water and restaurants developed, with tourists allowed to view the fish and select some for cooking in the restaurant. Tourism could provide the impetus for using more appropriate fishing techniques.

Building Standards

The plan recommends that maximum building heights for tourist facilities be established outside of urban areas. These would be four floors and 16 metres for high density developments, and two floors and 10 metres for medium and low density areas. Building height is measured from the natural grade to the top of the roof.

The plan indicates that the overall architectural design of tourist facilities should conform to the environment and indigenous styles of the development area. However, the point is made that new buildings should not be just replicas of traditional houses, but should be inspired by traditional styles and adapted to the environmental situation. In this manner a contemporary vernacular style can evolve. The plan recommends that local building materials be utilised to the extent possible. Building materials should not dominate the natural landscape but rather complement it.

The plan considers standards for the design of signs. They should fit well into the environment and be constructed of local building materials. Signs should be informative and express prohibitory activities in a tactful manner. All proposed signs should be approved by the local authority.

Utility Facilities and Services

The plan makes recommendations for environmentally appropriate utility facilities and services. These include solid waste disposal, sewage treatment, water and electric power supply, drainage, fire protection and communications.

For solid waste disposal in coastal tourism areas, the waste should be sorted, with biodegradable material deposited in a local sanitary landfill that is covered immediately after disposal. Non-biodegradable waste should be taken to an inland landfill. On the development sites, all waste should be kept in covered receptacles and screened from view. Development of compost pits for the disposal of organic wastes should be encouraged. A centralised collection and disposal system should be organised for inorganic garbage. The sites for sanitary landfills should be carefully selected based on suitable criteria. Burning of waste should be regulated. The method of sewage treatment must be designed based on a thorough assessment of the site and soil characteristics.

The quality of water supply should adhere to the national water code. When water is pumped from the ground, pumping tests should be conducted periodically to ensure that there is not over-extraction of groundwater. Electric power generation facilities should be designed to reduce noise levels. Electrical installations should meet the national electrical code. Drainage systems for dirty and storm water should be properly designed. Storm water may be drained into the sea, but dirty water such as from laundry use should be filtered before being allowed to drain into the sea. Fire protection facilities and services must be developed, and fire water hydrants installed. All resorts, even in remote areas, must have at least one means of outside communication.

Conclusions

The development standards and guidelines for the Philippines are comprehensive. Virtually all the important types are considered. The site planning considerations include the important factors of maintaining the natural features and appearance of the development sites. Establishment of buffer zones around the sites helps give them a separate 'sense of place', protects them from any undesirable nearby land uses and, in turn, protects nearby land uses from any intrusiveness of the tourism development.

The setbacks required from coastlines and beaches are critically important in order to preserve the natural shoreline appearance and ecological processes, and protect buildings from possible erosion and wave damage. These setbacks also provide better public access along the shore. Setbacks between buildings provide for greater privacy of the building occupants, and allow for landscaping among the buildings which enhances the appearance of the site. Establishing maximum building densities is an essential standard to maintain the desired character of the development, whether it is designed to be at a higher or lower intensity of use.

The requirement for a landscape plan is very appropriate in order to give greater assurance that proper landscaping will be carried out. The landscaping approach of preserving existing trees and using trees and other plants for various functional, as well as aesthetic, purposes follows good landscaping practices. The requirement for environmental impact assessments of proposed projects is very important in any tourism area.

The concern expressed in the plan about damage to the marine environment, especially from fish dynamiting, identifies a common and serious problem in many tropical countries. Also, a common problem in many places is removal of coral from the reefs for use in construction. The marine habitat is a very vulnerable one, easily degraded by misuse. It is also a type of environment that, when damaged, cannot be restored in a short period of time. Besides its importance to tourism, the marine environment serves essential ecological functions. Reefs, for example, protect the shore from wave erosion and provide a habitat for many organisms. The proposal made in the plan for developing alternative means of fishing, in order to stop dynamiting, is a practical and humane one. It recognises the need for fishermen to maintain their livelihood in an alternative manner.

The building design standards and architectural guidelines are reasonable ones. The valid point is made that contemporary building design need not exactly imitate traditional styles. Rather, the traditional design character, along with environmental considerations, can be incorporated into somewhat new styles that are still unique to the area. The emphasis on use of local building materials is very relevant because this helps integrate new buildings into the cultural and natural environment. Use of local materials also generates more economic benefits to the area through the production and sale of these materials for the construction of tourist facilities. The plan recognises that signs in tourism areas should be suitably designed to reflect the local environment, and be informative to tourists.

The recommendations made on utility facilities and services are important. Infrastructure should be developed to standards that will prevent any environmental problems being generated by tourism development.

The standards and guidelines presented here are those which are appropriate for coastal resort type development in somewhat remote areas. Although the same types of standards and guidelines would be applied everywhere, the specific standards and guidelines might be somewhat different for other kinds of tourism development.

24

Community Tourism Programme in Sri Lanka

The community tourism programme of the Sri Lanka plan represents an effective approach to involving local communities in the tourism development process. Through this involvement, communities can gain more benefits from tourism, and any adverse socio-cultural impacts can be lessened.

Background

The background of the Sri Lanka tourism plan was described in a previous case study, and so is only summarised here. Sri Lanka is located off the southeastern tip of India. The country has varied mountain and coastal geography and a tropical climate. Sri Lanka has a population of 17.2 million, composed of Sinhalese, Tamils and other groups. There is a great diversity of attractions for tourists. These range from beaches and marine environments, national parks with forests and wildlife, outstanding archaeological and historic sites and interesting cultural patterns to tea plantations, spice gardens and gem mines. Tourism was substantially developed from the 1960s to the early 1980s. Then internal civil strife led to a marked decline of tourist arrivals and some deterioration of tourist facilities.

Since 1990, tourism has recovered rapidly and there were some 320,000 international tourist arrivals in 1991. Tourist facilities are being rehabilitated and new investments in tourism development are being proposed. Most tourism is based on beach-oriented accommodation, although some tourism development exists in the inland areas where most of the natural and cultural attractions are located.

The tourism plan of Sri Lanka was prepared in 1992 (UNDP and WTO, 1992. *Sri Lanka Tourism Master Plan.* Madrid: WTO). This is a comprehensive plan that examines all aspects of tourism. The tourism development strategy is four-fold—diversify the tourist market mix; increase tourist spending by developing and upgrading tourist facilities; diversify tourist attractions by emphasising development and promotion of cultural, natural and other types of feature; and create a positive image of the country. An optimum market target of 874,000 international tourist arrivals is established for 2001. A doubling of the average daily tourist expenditure is projected. The plan also makes recommendations on domestic tourism.

The development strategy identifies 14 tourism zones throughout the country. Within these zones, the plan proposes upgrading of existing development in a coordinated manner and initiation of major new planned integrated tourism developments. The strategy emphasises providing a diversity of tourist attractions and related small-scale tourism development. New and expanded tour routes are recommended. Elements of the plan are focused on environmental and social issues and enhancing the economic benefits of tourism. Part of the consideration on social and economic issues is encouraging more involvement of communities in the tourism development of their local areas.

Community Tourism Programme

As stated in the plan, community tourism seeks to balance community aspirations with the type and pace of tourism development undertaken, in order to ensure that all community interests are represented. Several approaches are recommended to achieve community involvement in tourism. These are described in the following paragraphs.

In areas of tourist resorts or where substantial tourism activity exists or is proposed, tourism committees should be established. These committees would be composed of representatives of community interests, local police, tourism-related businesses, other business interest directly or indirectly affected by tourism, social and community liaison workers assigned to tourism projects and local government officials. The committees would receive technical and organisational support from Ceylon Tourist Board (CTB)—the national statutory tourism organisation.

When setting up the committees, there should be a public relations campaign to inform local residents of what to expect in tourism development, and how to take advantage of the new business coming to their area. The local socio-cultural issues on tourism would also be addressed in this public information programme. After being established, the committees should first decide the objectives of tourism in the area and agree on a set of policies and principles that should be adhered to.

The main functions of the committees would be as follows :

- Solicit proposals for tourism projects from the community.
- Act as consultative bodies for tourism development proposals in the area.
- Identify and raise any issues relating to local tourism operations.
- Instigate arbitration of conflicts arising between the community and tourism industry within the area.
- Instigate initiatives benefiting tourism and the community.

In each area of high social vulnerability where major tourism projects are proposed, a tourism community liaison officer should be appointed by the tourism committee. The officer's salary would be borne by the developer of the tourism project. A liaison officer should also be appointed in areas of existing tourism activity where problems exist or are anticipated. Training of these officers will be required on community issues related to tourism. The CTB would provide this training. The officer should represent the interests of the community, including low income and socially vulnerable groups. The officer would coordinate with the CTB or other organisations to meet special training needs, for example on trade skills or small business management. Public health and AIDS awareness would also be addressed by the officer.

The local hotel associations should be committed to working with the local tourism committees, to their mutual advantage. Policies should be drafted to include ways in which the local communities can benefit directly from tourist spending, and indirectly through supplying the hotels and other tourism enterprises with goods and services. Hoteliers should also help communicate local codes of behaviour and social traditions to their guests.

Guest houses and informal accommodation units are the interface where many social problems arising from meeting of tourists and residents begin. The tourism liaison officers should work closely with the owners and managers of these establishments. These owners and managers should become involved in AIDS awareness programmes and be encouraged to participate in and circulate community information. They should also become involved with the activities of the tourism committees.

Tour operators (both national and local) should commit themselves to respect and promote local culture and small business in the areas in which they operate. Furthermore, they should establish guidelines on their own operations. These guidelines would cover various activities—taking tourists to designated handicraft centres where small businesses operate; passing on information about the socio-cultural policies of Sri Lanka; and informing and encouraging tourists to respect local cultural standards.

Community tourism centres should be set up in resorts, as places where both tourists and residents can obtain information and buy and sell local products. The centres should be centrally located in the resorts. They should include a tourist information office, the office of the tourism liaison officer and retail shops. Encouragement should be given to establishing a branch of the tourist police in each resort area.

Conclusions

In many tourism areas—especially in the past—local community involvement in tourism was neglected as being too troublesome and expensive for government or business to support. However, lack of community involvement has led to problems in some tourism areas. These problems have related both to adverse socio-cultural impacts on the communities and the local residents not having the opportunity to participate in and receive economic benefits from tourism development in their areas.

The proposals made in the Sri Lanka plan reflect a sound approach to achieving community involvement. Establishing local tourism committees composed of all the relevant parties will provide focal points for discussion and action. Appointing tourism liaison officers in critical tourism areas will provide the additional focus needed in those places to resolve problems and offer assistance. The financial support for these officers by the resorts is justified—the resorts receive benefits from having good community relations and they have a responsibility to assist their communities.

Especially important is the approach of giving responsibility to the local tourism enterprises—applying measures that will prevent social problems from arising and encouraging development, and use of other local businesses and community handicraft centres. A common problem in many tourism areas is tourists being guided to shops that may pay the guide a high commission, but do not greatly benefit the local business community. Without the support and initiative of tourism enterprises, the community tourism programme could not be successful.

Setting up community tourism centres is a well established technique to disseminate information and provide local entrepreneurs with a central place from which to sell their products. Making tourist police available in resorts is also a recognised technique, not only to enforce local regulations but also to give information and a sense of security to tourists.

After government adoption of these community tourism proposals, the next step is implementation. This will require organisational initiative, technical assistance and some funding—at least for training and perhaps also for making loans to establish local small tourism businesses. The funding could be provided jointly by the government (national or local) and the local private section.

Often a successful implementation technique is to organise one or two demonstration projects. Such projects can provide the basis for refining techniques, and they serve as prototypes for other communities to organise their programmes. The CTB, along with the provincial or district governments, could serve as the catalyst for initiating these demonstration community tourism projects. The local communities, however, will need to be very supportive of and actively participate in the projects in order for them to be successful.

25

Tourism Plan for Ambergris Caye, Belize

The master plan for Ambergris Caye in Belize is an example of integrated planning for a tourism-based island community. Planning is directed toward preserving the community's distinctive informal character, while still allowing for the controlled growth of tourism.

Background

The country of Belize is located in Central America fronting on the Caribbean Sea. It shares a boundary with Guatemala on the west and the Yucatan Peninsula of Mexico on the north. The population of about 180,000 is primarily English speaking with Spanish also widely used. Belize City, situated on the coast, is the main urban centre. The planned and relatively new town of Belmopan, located inland, is now the country's capital. Offshore, and part of Belize, is the Western Hemisphere's longest barrier reef. On this reef are several islands or cayes, of which the largest is Ambergris Caye in the north.

Tourism in Belize has grown rapidly in recent years—from 94,000 international arrivals in 1986 to 222,000 arrivals in 1990. However, many of these arrivals come on short-stay border crossings from the neighbouring countries. In 1990, some 80,000 tourists arrived by air. Most tourists are from the USA and Canada, with much lesser numbers from the UK and other countries in Europe.

Tourism in Belize has been—and still is—focused on beach and marine activities, combined with the pleasant sub-tropical climate. Sport fishing and diving are especially popular. The main tourism development is on Ambergris Caye, concentrated in and near the main town of San Pedro. Recently the country has also been developing nature tourism, based particularly on the scenic mountains and wildlife of the southern area of the country. Some land and marine conservation areas have been designated. Belize also possesses several Mayan archaeological sites, some of which are accessible and visited by tourists. *La Ruta Maya* (The Mayan Route) links several of the Mayan sites in Belize with those of the nearby countries of Mexico, Guatemala, Honduras and El Salvador. This forms a 2,400 kilometre road network of accessible archaeological sites in Central America.

Planning Approach

Although the main tourism centre of Ambergris Caye was functioning reasonably well in the late 1980s, there was concern that continued uncontrolled development would be detrimental to the island's environmental and social character. At the same time, certain improvements were required to the existing development patterns, especially in San Pedro. Consequently, the master plan for Ambergris Caye was prepared to guide the island's future development (UNDP and WTO, 1989. *Ambergris Caye Master Development and Zoning Plan—Belize.* Madrid: WTO). This plan comprises three major components :

- The development strategy, which deals with the entire island.
- The San Pedro District plan, which is detailed land use planning of the San Pedro town area.
- The institutional framework, which outlines ways to facilitate implementation of the master plan.

The planning approach is quite comprehensive. It considers overall community as well as tourism development needs in an integrated manner. A planning appraisal was conducted of several elements—population and employment; physical and environmental characteristics; San Pedro town; communications (road, air and sea transport); public utilities (water supply, sewage and solid waste disposal, electric power and telecommunications); and a legislative and institutional overview. A summary was made of major problems and opportunities. Tourism on Ambergris Caye was reviewed with respect to several factors—the national context;

general characteristics; specific tourism statistics; tourist attractions; and accommodation and other tourist facilities. Extensive field surveys were carried out and meetings held with government agencies, the private sector and community leaders. The plans were prepared to a time scale from 1988 to 2005, with intermediate periods established for 1990, 1995 and 2000.

The key development objectives are set forth in the plan as follows :

- Provide opportunities for the future natural expansion of tourism in keeping with the general character, environment and the unspoilt nature of the island.
- Generate jobs for the future natural increase of the resident population, as a minimum level of jobs needed.
- Maintain as far as possible the existing character of urban and rural environments.
- Protect sensitive ecologies from excessive human activity.
- Avoid levels of immigration that put an undue social strain on the community or its facilities.
- Plan for the ordered expansion of San Pedro town to meet existing and future population needs.
- Establish a context for the systematic planning and development of tourist accommodation and associated facilities.
- Inhibit speculation in and the high cost of land.

The plan states that, given these objectives, strategic options are limited. Development alternatives mainly revolve around the quantity of tourism development and its consequent impact, with a balancing of social and economic costs and benefits. Too little growth would not take advantage of the potential benefits to be gained from increases in employment and foreign currency earnings. Too much growth would involve excessive rates of immigration and impose intolerable burdens on the community, the environment and social infrastructure. The preferred option seeks to control the expansion of tourism to be at a similar rate and form to that experienced in the recent past. It continues the image of a relaxed, small-scale, informal tourism community that has been so successful, and which residents and visitors both prefer.

Master Plan

The island-wide development strategy comprises several elements—the programme for tourist accommodation; employment and population; land use strategy; and infrastructure. The plan estimates that, by 1990, existing and committed accommodation development will be 500 hotel rooms and 100 apartments or houses for rent to tourists. The accommodation development rate is recommended to be controlled, producing a total of about 1,200 hotel rooms by 2005. The maximum size of hotels is recommended to be no more than 60 rooms—in keeping with the objective of maintaining the small to medium scale character of the resort community. The remaining new accommodation would be in the form of about 250 rental apartments and housing units. Also 500 retirement and vacation homes are projected for development by 2005—retirement and vacation home development by expatriates was already commencing on Ambergris in the late 1980s.

The plan states that this is considered to be a modest programme, in relation to market expectations, but it should be regarded as the maximum level of acceptable development. Even this programme is conditional upon developing new sources of potable water supply. At this level of development, visitors to Ambergris are likely to increase from between 10,000 and 12,500 in 1988 to between 69,000 and 89,000 in 2005, depending on the average length of stay. Tourist expenditures are estimated to rise from an annual US $ 11 million in 1990 to US $ 37 million in 2005 (at constant prices). The plan indicates that, even with a substantial leakage out of Belize (for imported goods used in tourism), the recommended programme will still make a substantial net contribution to the economy and foreign exchange.

The plan projects that the 2005 level of development will generate an additional 4,000 jobs, for a total of 5,000 persons employed in tourism by that year. Slightly over 80 per cent of these jobs can be filled by Belizeans. This is in keeping with the objective of minimising immigration. However, reaching that level of Belizean employment will require special efforts—tighter immigration controls; training citizens to properly assume tourism positions; and establishing the right conditions, such as good housing and schools, to attract some Belizeans from the mainland to live and work on Ambergris.

Based on the growth of employment, the plan projects the population of the island to increase at a rate of nearly 10 per cent per year—from 2,600 in 1988 to 12,700 in 2005. After allowing for the natural growth of the present population, there will be a need for about 7,400 Belizean and 1,350 non-Belizean migrants to the island. The plan emphasises that assimilating these migrants will be a major task, including providing more school facilities.

The land use development strategy set forth in the plan is shown in Figure 25.1. This strategy consists of five key elements, as follows :

- Reservation of the whole of the northern part of the island to be kept in its natural condition.
- Definition of three specific conservation areas (in addition to an existing marine reserve).
- Restriction of development on the east coast to a specific area.
- Expansion and consolidation of San Pedro within a specific area.
- Establishment, in the medium to longer-term, of a new settlement in the centre of the island.

The strategy includes development on the east coast of three low density resorts consisting of several beach-front hotels of about 60 rooms each. These would be associated with an equivalent area of residential tourism subdivisions. Each resort should be comprehensively planned in partnership between the owners and planning authorities. Each resort would have a small commercial and entertainment centre, and provide lots for housing of employees. Each hotel would be allowed to develop one pier that should be open to the public and nearby residential tourists. Public access would be provided to the beach at intervals of no more than 300 metres. A similar nuclear resort would be developed on the west coast.

The plan specifies various types of land use zones—suburban hotels (150 beds per hectare); rural hotels (50 beds per hectare); residential tourism outside of San Pedro (two densities of 5 and 10 houses per hectare), nature reserves; conservation zones; and Special Coordinated Development Areas (SCDAs). The SCDAs

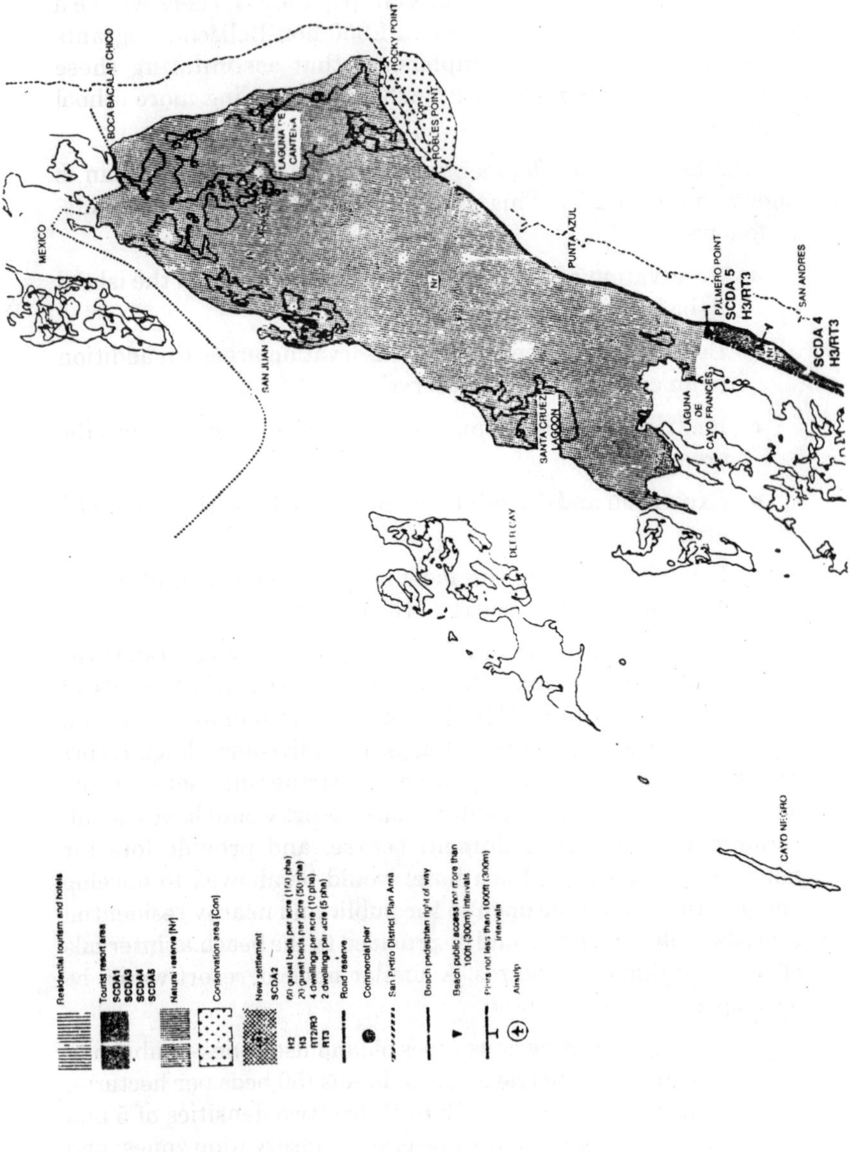
MEXICO
BOCA BACALAR CHICO
LAGUNA DE CANTENA
ROCKY POINT
ROBLES POINT
PUNTA AZUL
PALMERO POINT
SCDA 5
H3/RT3
SAN ANDRES
SCDA 4
H3/RT3
SAN JUAN
SANTA CRUZ LAGOON
LAGUNA DE CAYO FRANCES
DEER CAY
CAYO NEGRO
Residential tourism and hotels
Tourist resort area
SCDA1
SCDA3
SCDA4
SCDA5
Natural reserve [Nr]
Conservation area [Con]
New settlement
SCDA2
Road reserve
Commercial pier
San Pedro District Plan Area
Beach pedestrian right of way
Airstrip

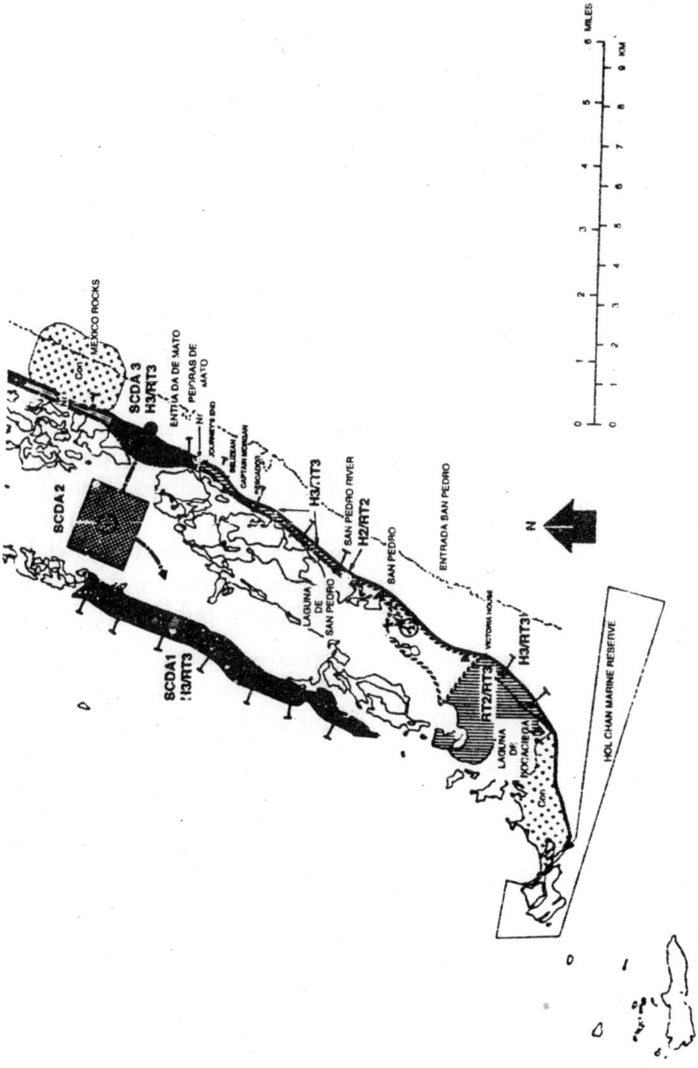

Fig 25.1 : Ambergris Caye master plan.

are places which are required to be planned comprehensively and the development closely coordinated. There are five such areas shown on the plan—four resort areas and the new settlement in the centre of the island.

Recommendations are made on the infrastructure development of the airport, roads, water supply and other utility services. The plan states that, if a new potable groundwater supply cannot be found, it will be necessary to instal a desalination plant.

The Sen Pedro district plan is a detailed land use and zoning plan. The present town area is expanded north and south of the traditional core to provide for a total resident population of 8,000, as well as sites for new hotels, holiday condominiums and subdivisions for retirement and vacation homes. The plan states that San Pedro will increasingly perform the function of the island's urban centre—it will be the main focus of commercial activities, services to tourists, high density hotels and guest houses, and self-catering apartments. This consolidation will be effected by changes in the use of existing buildings, the development of vacant sites and the renewal of outworn buildings. Specific recommendations are made for the different types of land use areas, the road network and dredging of the river, with development of a storm-sheltered commercial harbour and marina. Improvements are recommended to social and public facilities.

In order to maintain the present small-scale and pedestrian-oriented urban quality and character of San Pedro, the plan sets forth urban design guidelines. Building heights are restricted to two storeys, except in two areas where three storeys will be allowed if there is commensurate open space allocated on the building sites. Building form will be confined to traditional designs—finished in timber cladding, painted white, and having open balustraded verandahs and low-pitched roofs. Different types of land use zones are specified for the town. More detailed planning is presented for the central area of San Pedro—the Town Centre Action Area Plan and, within that area, the town plaza development proposals scheme. The San Pedro Plan makes recommendations on all the infrastructure elements.

The report states that, 'The master plan will be of little use unless machinery is established for, and the resources devoted to its management and implementation'. It makes several recommendations on the institutional framework for implementing the island development strategy and San Pedro land use plan. The master plan is expressed in the form of a Planning Scheme for Ambergris Caye under the Housing and Planning ordinance. The adoption of this scheme, alongwith its accompanying maps (the island-wide Development Strategy Map and the San Pedro District Plan Map), will provide the statutory basis for enforcing the master plan. The responsible ministry will then be in a position to set up an Ambergris Caye Planning Authority to oversee implementation of the plan. The Authority would be composed of representatives of the concerned agencies, and a member nominated by the San Pedro Town Board.

The planning authority will need to establish a technical staff to advise on its actions. The technical staff will have three primary responsibilities—receiving and evaluating development proposals; monitoring development and residential subdivisions; and modifying the plan in the face of changing circumstances.

The plan examines the serious problem of land speculation on Ambergris. It attributes this problem to the lack of development controls and adequate restrictions on the sale of land to foreigners. Adoption and implementation of the plan will establish the appropriate development controls. On sale of land to foreigners, the plan recommends that any foreign land sale must be approved by the appropriate Ministry, and that no more than 50 per cent of any residential subdivision be allowed to be sold to foreigners. In this way, an assured number of land plots would become available for the use of citizens at a price which reflects the local market value among citizens. As appendix of the plan report sets forth the detailed legal regulations for the Ambergris Caye Planning Scheme. After review and any necessary modifications are made the regulations can be adopted by the government.

The plan recommends on several other specific needs—deep drilling to try to locate a new potable water source; conducting a feasibility study for improvement of the airfield; designs for liquid waste stabilisation ponds and a solid waste disposal site; purchase of land and design for a new primary school; and reservation of a new road alignment.

Conclusions

The Ambergris Caye planning study takes a comprehensive approach to planning for a resort island community. Emphasis is placed on maintaining the small-scale and informal character of the community, while still allowing for substantial increases in tourism and the resident population. The plan rightfully does not try to emulate more structured resort development elsewhere. Ambergris offers a distinctive environment for residents, that also satisfies particular market segments, and it would be a mistake to try to change this special ambience. This approach, however, implies highly controlled development in the face of rapidly growing market demand.

Controlled development can be achieved in Ambergris because Belize has ample opportunity to develop other tourism areas elsewhere in the country, based on beach, marine, nature and archaeological tourism resources. Development of tourism elsewhere has several advantages—diversifying the tourism product and tourist markets; spreading economic benefits more widely; and providing incentives for conservation of natural areas and archaeological sites.

In the planning process, the plan examines all the necessary influencing factors—the natural environment; urban and tourism land use patterns; the society and economy; and the infrastructure. Utmost consideration is given to conservation needs in the plan. This is important for both the success of tourism and benefit of residents. Sound planning principles are applied of concentrating accommodation and other tourist facilities in certain areas, as well as consolidating town development. Eventual development of a new settlement in the centre of the island will help absorb the additional population, while maintaining the tightly-knit character of San Pedro. Establishing controls on the maximum size of new hotels and on development character, such as height limits, are appropriate techniques. These controls can help retain the desired small-scale character of both community and tourism development.

The plan establishes the specific implementation mechanisms and procedures that need to be followed. By setting forth, in the appendix, the legal regulations for the Ambergris Caye Planning Scheme, the government is given precise legislation which it can adopt directly from the report, if it wishes. Continuous control and management of development will be essential to achieve the plan's concepts and recommendations.

26

Travel Facilitation in the Ethiopia Tourism

The recommendations made in the national tourism plan of Ethiopia for improving travel facilitation requirements and procedures for tourists represent those that are applicable to many countries. Efficient travel facilitation is essential for the substantial development of tourism.

Background

Ethiopia is situated in East Africa, north of Kenya, south of Eritrea and between Sudan on the west and Somalia and Djibouti on the east. The country has a wide range of environmental zones and associated wildlife and vegetation. Highlands with elevations of more than 2,000 metres extend over much of the central parts of the country. There are still some coniferous forests above the 3,000 metre level but most of the highlands have been cleared for agriculture. Lowland regions surround the highlands with semi-arid and arid climatic and vegetation patterns. The rift valley and its several lakes lie in the south-central part of the country—this valley extends through several eastern and southern African countries. Lake Tana, in the northwest, is the source of the Blue Nile.

Ethiopia has a long history extending through thousands of years. It is referred to in ancient Egyptian texts and was an early centre of Christianity in Africa. The country was never colonised except for a brief period from 1936–41. The present population of about 50 million is composed mostly of farmers and herders. The capital of Addis Ababa, with some 1.5 million inhabitants, is an attractive city located in the central highlands. Addis is the seat of the Organisation of African Unity and the United Nations Economic Commission for Africa, and is the regional headquarters for other international organisations. In recent years, the country has been troubled by internal political disturbances and famine. These have been a serious deterrent to both tourism and general development.

The country possesses substantial resources for tourism. There is a diversity of scenic areas and wildlife (including many types of large animals and abundant birdlife) related to the different environmental zones. Some wildlife species are unique to the country. Several national parks and nature reserves have been designated and conservation programmes are underway. However, certain animal species require further conservation efforts to be fully rejuvenated. The largest concentrations of wildlife exist in the southwestern corner of the country near the border with Kenya and Sudan. The second major type of attraction is the many archaeological and historical sites, notably the rock-hewn churches at Lalibela, remains of the 2,000 year-old Auxmite Empire and medieval monasteries at Lake Tana, found particularly in the northern areas of the country. Because of the extensive tropical highland environment, the climate is generally pleasant throughout the year.

During the late 1980s to 1990, Ethiopia received somewhat more than 70,000 tourist arrivals annually. Only about 20 per cent of these were holiday tourists and the remainder were business travellers or in transit. Several thousand of the arrivals are coming to attend international association meetings being held in Addis. Controlled hunting tourism is allowed. Although not attracting a large number of tourists, hunting is a very high value form of tourism that generates considerable revenue. Foreigners living in the country provide an important source of 'domestic' tourists visiting the national parks and historic sites. There have been several constraints on developing tourism—the limited supply and quality of tourist facilities and services; attractions that are spread over large areas and, in some places, poorly linked by transportation services; and the negative international image of the country because of political disturbances and famine.

Tourism Planning Approach

The national tourism plan was prepared for Ethiopia in 1990 (UNDP and WTO, 1990. *National Tourism Development Plan of Ethiopia. Vols. I, II and III.* Madrid: WTO). This was a comprehensive planning programme. However, because of security problems prevailing in some parts of the country at the time of plan preparation, the planning programme focused primarily on the southern region. It includes the structure plan, a five-year action programme, master planning of three tourism priority areas and detailed plans and prefeasibility analyses of priority tourism development sites. The national plan is prepared for 1989–2005 and encompasses several elements—designation of tourism development regions; tour patterns and programmes; economic cost and benefit analysis; environmental impact with recommended conservation measures and development and design standards; socio-cultural impact evaluation; manpower planning and training programmes; recommendations on organisational structures and legislation; and an implementation strategy and need for monitoring implementation. The action programme includes physical development projects, other actions needed and a marketing strategy to implement the first stage of the tourism plan.

A three-step methodological approach is applied in formulating the plan. The first step is a review of the country's characteristics and the overall national development policy including existing policies for developing tourism. Then the tourism supply is surveyed and evaluated. This includes several elements—existing and potential natural and cultural tourist attractions and activities; access to the country, internal transportation facilities and services and other infrastructure; accommodation, catering and entertainment; and technical resources such as organisation, commercial, training and financial factors. Lastly, the tourism demand is analysed. This involves a detailed analysis of each of the domestic and international tourist flows. Demand forecasts are made on the basis of quantitative and qualitative considerations, and include tourist arrivals and their characteristics and the future need for accommodation by location and type. The tourism image of the country is considered, and possible competitive destinations are reviewed. Substantial increases in the numbers of tourist arrivals are targeted for the future.

In planning the priority tourism areas, calculation of their carrying capacities was an important consideration in determining the type and level of development.

The planning analysis concludes that the country's strong points for tourism are its impressive natural and cultural attractions which can be related to sight-seeing, educational, special interest and adventure tour groups. The plan designates Addis Ababa as the tourism gateway and staging area and ten tourism development zones. Seven of these zones are shown as priority development areas. One of the priority zones is identified as weekend areas for trips from Addis. The action programme recommends that, in addition to some existing historical tour routes, new areas should be opened soon which include circuits of game parks. These are located in the southern part of the country.

The number and type of accommodation rooms are allocated to each of the zones. Some of these units are recommended to be in the form of 'ecological habitations (ecohabs)'. These are detached units built from local materials in the regional architectural styles. They could be located within national parks and reserves because they do not interfere with the natural environment. Other types of accommodation—'bungalow parks'—would be constructed outside the parks. Accommodation would also be substantially expanded, in Addis, with new hotel developed. As the country's tourism gateway and conference and commercial centre, the capital will continue attracting large numbers of holiday and business tourists.

Travel Facilitation Recommendations

The Ethiopia plan makes specific recommendations on measures to facilitate tourists travelling to and within the country. It first identifies the obstacles affecting individual tourists visiting the country, including the following :

- Currency restrictions imposed upon visitors.
- Entry visas, identity documents and limitation on duration of stay.
- Formalities concerning entry of motor vehicles.

- Formalities concerning applicability of drivers' licences, car insurance, etc.

The plan explains that the requirement that entry visas of all visitors (except from Kenya and Djibouti) be obtained before arrival is a deterrent to encouraging tourism. However, the plan recognises that there was the need to control entry carefully in the past. It recommends that, in the future, visas be issued on the arrival of tourists, and that visas be valid for multiple entries. Within the country, the plan recommends that internal travel be liberalised to the extent possible. The plan also describes the complications entailed in tourists completing the currency forms and maintaining records of currency transactions. It points out that this requirement should be investigated.

On entry procedures at the international airport, the plan indicates that the procedures are confusing and time-consuming. It recommends several ways to improve entry facilitation at the airport, as follows :

- Clear entry instructions should be printed in several languages informing arrivals that they must go through (1) immigration, including passport examination, (2) currency control, and (3) customs.
- Explicit instructions should be given to tourists concerning the necessity to produce a record of currency transactions on departure.

The plan states that the airport terminal still has enough space to handle a moderate increase in traffic, but the efficiency of handling tourists could be improved. It recommends several approaches :

- A system of directional signs should be installed to ensure a smoother flow of arrivals and departures.
- Customs and immigration procedures should be adapted to the potential importance of tourism to Ethiopia's economy (that is, efficient and courteous).
- The language barrier for tourists is a serious one. This applies to both officials and the staff on duty at the airport building. As a first step, the installation of multi-lingual signs listing vital information would do much to alleviate this situation.

- There are no posters or photographs to acquaint the tourist or in-transit passenger with the attractions of Addis Ababa and Ethiopia. A simple information pamphlet in one or two colours would be informative for the arriving tourist or in-transit passenger.

The plan indicates that Ethiopia has no airport departure tax as do most other countries. It recommends that, as tourism expands in the future, the introduction of a departure tax would provide revenue that could help finance the promotional budget of the country in its marketing of tourism.

On internal travel facilitation and transportation improvements, the plan makes several recommendations. It indicates that automobile tourism could be expanded in the future. Maximum advantage should be taken of using the existing road system, which is quite good in some areas, for tourist travel. Car rental services should be competitively priced to encourage individual auto travel. The plan makes recommendations on ways to improve domestic air travel for tourists, bus services throughout the country and taxicab services in the urban areas. To encourage tourist use of the railway system, the plan recommends that first class coaches be introduced in the future for tourist use to specific places.

Recommendations are also made on improving the number and quality of local tour guides. This should include training of the guides in more foreign languages.

The plan notes that credit cards are widely used by tourists everywhere, and that facilitating use of credit cards in Ethiopia would provide an important convenience to tourists and they would increase their spending. It recommends that the tourism office encourage the acceptance and use of credit cards by operators of hotels and other tourist services and, if necessary, make the appropriate arrangements with monetary control authorities.

The plan states that directives on improving various aspects of travel facilitation should be decided at government level. The tourism office should have the responsibility of coordinating with the appropriate agencies in implementing the improvements.

Conclusions

The Ethiopia tourism planning programme is a comprehensive one that uses a systematic methodological approach. It examines the overall characteristics of the country, including the institutional elements, as the basis for planning; it analyses the tourism supply of existing tourist facilities, services and infrastructure, existing and potential tourist attractions and activities and the technical resources for development, and it analyses the tourist demand in detail. Particular attention is given to inventory and evaluation of tourism resources. The principle of establishing tourism development zones and prioritising development of these zones is applied. The action programme sets forth the requirements for implementing the first stage of development.

Among other considerations, the plan emphasises the importance of improving travel facilitation requirements and procedures for tourists. On a global basis, encouraging travel facilitation improvements has been a significant programme of the World Tourism Organisation for several years. These improvements are essential for facilitating international travel among different countries—they are especially needed in countries which are commencing to develop tourism. At the same time, it is recognised that all countries must maintain some controls on entry of visitors and goods.

In the Ethiopia plan, the importance of providing visas on arrival, at least from the major tourist market countries, is emphasised as a basic facilitation improvement. Also the plan makes the valid point that the overall entry procedures at the international airport should be efficient and courteous, and the necessary information provided. Providing efficient entry procedures is also, of course, applicable to any international entry point including land border crossings and seaports. The convenience experienced by tourists when they enter a country forms their first, and often lasting, impression of the destination. In many countries needing entry improvements, an approach commonly used is to organise sensitivity training courses for airport officials, especially those in immigration and customs, so that they better understand how to handle arriving tourists.

The recommendation for establishing an airport departure tax is a valid one. Departure taxes are required in many countries. This tax can provide an important source of revenue for the government, especially if it is used to improve and promote tourism in some manner. However, the departure tax should not be so high as to irritate tourists.

To facilitate travel within the country, the recommendation to make it easier for tourists to rent cars will encourage more individual automobile travel. This will broaden the tourist markets, extend their average length of stay and bring some benefits of tourism to places that otherwise might not be visited by tourists. Facilitating use of credit cards by tourists is now a major consideration in any tourism area.

The plan justifiably identifies the tourism office as being the logical responsible agency for coordinating facilitation improvements. However, many of the actual improvements must be undertaken by the various other agencies involved. Because of the complexity of entry procedures, it is common practice in many countries to establish a permanent travel facilitation committee. This committee is composed of representatives of all the concerned government agencies and autonomous boards or authorities. It has the responsibility to recommend improvements needed to facilitation requirements and procedures, and to monitor the effectiveness of facilitation activities.

27

Implementation Manual in the Uganda Tourism

The implementation manual in the Uganda tourism plan sets forth a systematic and specific procedure for adopting and maintaining the tourism plan and development programme.

Background

The background of Uganda was described in a previous case study, and so is only summarised here. Uganda is located in east-central Africa, inland from Kenya. The country has a population of about 17 million and includes several cultural groups. The capital city of Kampala has about half a million inhabitants. The primary attractions for tourists are outstanding scenic areas, including lakes, rivers, mountains, rainforests and savanna, and a variety of wildlife. Important specific features include Murchison Falls, the Ruwenzori Mountains and mountain gorilla reserves. Ten national parks have been designated in the country although most of these still have limited tourist facilities. The upland climate is very pleasant for tourists.

Tourism was relatively well developed in Uganda in the late 1960s and early 1970s. Then, because of political turmoil and changes in government policy, tourism became virtually non-existent. Much of the tourist facility development and infrastructure was damaged or deteriorated from lack of maintenance. Since the mid-1980s, rehabilitation of the country's economy has been taking place, including of tourism development. Major conservation programmes are being implemented to rejuvenate the wildlife. Substantial progress has been made on rehabilitation, and game populations are recovering, but these programmes are still underway.

The government policy is now for revitalisation of the tourism sector as an important source of economic development. Tourism is also seen as a means to achieve conservation objectives. In 1991, Uganda received 68,000 international tourist arrivals. Only about 10,000 of these arrivals were holiday tourists, with the remainder coming for business, official mission and other purposes. Most of the holiday arrivals were budget types of tourists. The large international aid community in Uganda provides many of the present visitors to the national parks.

In the early 1990s, a tourism plan was prepared for Uganda (UNDP and WTO, 1993. *Integrated Tourism Master Plan—Republic of Uganda. Vols. I, II and III.* Madrid: WTO). The planning approach is comprehensive, and examines all aspects of tourism. The development strategy emphasises that tourist market development must take place slowly because tourist facilities and the wildlife will remain rather limited for the next few years. The spatial development concept is based on establishment of tourism zones—three primary, two secondary and three tertiary zones. Several possible tourist circuits are identified which link the tourism zones. The plan recommends that tourist service centres be developed to provide tourist information, nature interpretation exhibits, tourism services, medical clinics and commercial facilities.

Implementation Manual

As part of the implementation section of the Uganda tourism plan, an implementation manual was set forth. This manual focuses on the procedure for adopting and maintaining the development plan and programme. The diagram in Figure 27.1 depicts the implementation procedure. Under the purpose section of the manual, it states that the National Structure Plan establishes the planning and policy strategy for the development of the tourism sector over the period of 1993 to 2002. This is translated into an Action and Development Programme of priority projects for the first five years. This programme is the foundation of the implementation process—it expresses the principles and phasing of the plan in terms of actual projects. These projects can then be allocated to an implementing body and budgeted for accordingly.

The manual makes recommendations on how to establish the authority and status of the tourism structure plan. It states that the plan must be given an authoritative status which can only come from Cabinet approval. This will involve a two-stage process. First, there should be approval in principle. An Inter-Ministry Coordination Committee should be established—this would be composed of senior representatives of all the ministries and agencies which are affected by the plan. The committee would review the proposed plan in detail, make any recommendations for modifications, and submit it to the cabinet for approval. This approval would be confined to basic planning and policy issues and would not extend to detail.

The second stage is general public and private sector participation. Following Cabinet approval, the structure plan should be published and made available for sale and inspection in libraries and schools, with press releases describing the plan. In districts that are particularly affected by the plan, public meetings could be organised. Dialogue would also be organised with the private sector interests in tourism. All serious comments on the plan would be assembled, and a report prepared that identifies any matters of substance for consideration of the Inter-Ministry Coordination Committee. Following deliberations by this committee, it would present its conclusions to the Cabinet for approval. Any agreed changes of importance could be published as an Addendum to the National Structure Plan.

The manual next sets forth the approval process for the Action and Development Programme. The manual states that this programme is composed of projects which are considered desirable and reasonably realistic to implement. The manual states, however, that the programme has wide-ranging implications on resources and budgets. Reaching agreement on the public sector commitments of the programme could be time-consuming and controversial.

The manual recommends that a small Development Programme Sub-Committee of the Inter-Ministry Coordination Committee be organised to review the proposed programme. It lists the organisations which should be represented on this Sub-

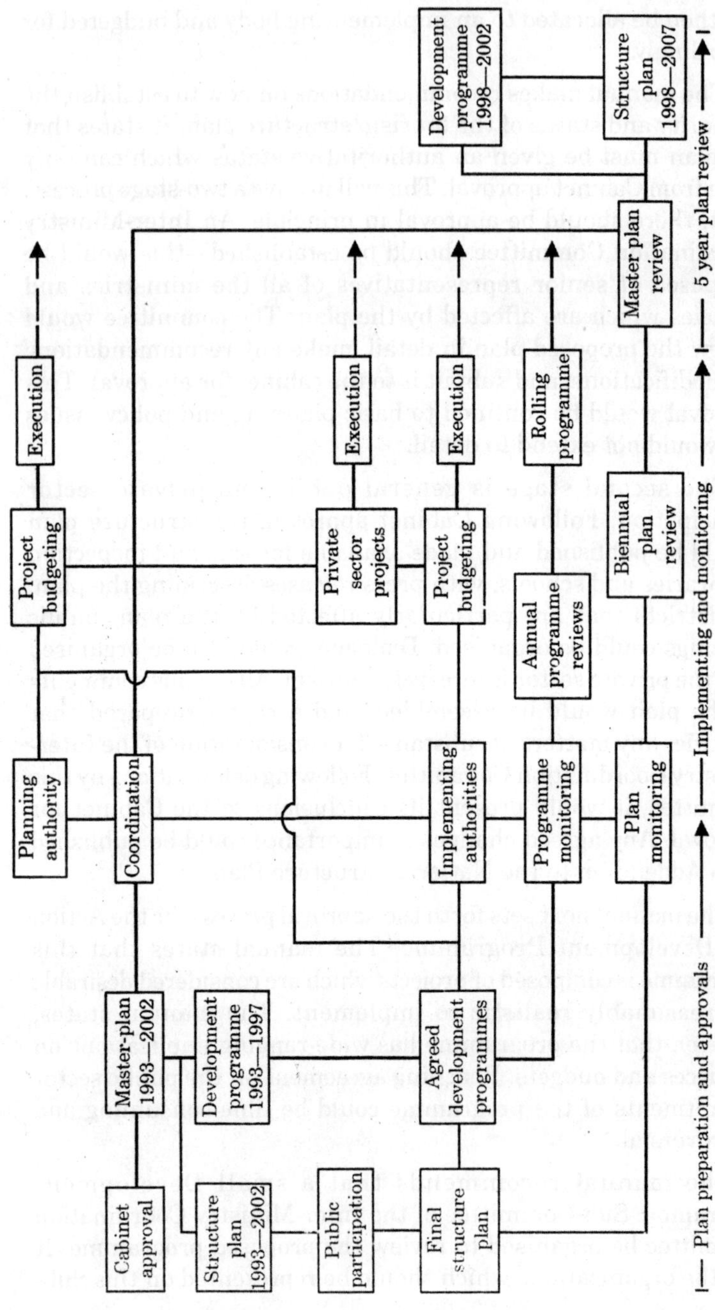

Fig 27.1 : Implementation diagram for the Uganda tourism plan.

Committee. The Sub-Committee would review the programme from a general standpoint, balancing the economic and social advantages of taking different courses of action. Then it would arrive at a mutually agreed programme. The manual indicates that any changes to the programme would likely relate to scheduling of projects, rather than to the specific projects included in the programme.

The manual then indicates that, using the agreed programme as a basis, the Ministry of Tourism would have the following tasks :

- Identify the executive implementing authorities for the different public sector projects.
- Inform them of their responsibilities in this regard.
- Prepare briefs on the specific policy action or project development required, and the proposed time of the action or project.

Following discussion with the respective implementing authorities on their programme obligations, any changes that might be required would be mutually agreed. The implementing authorities would then prepare the requisite budgets and submit these through the normal procedures for approval. They would then inform the Ministry of Tourism of the approved projects and budgets, and any amendments made. At the same time, they would identify potential aid-funded projects and relevant aid agencies. The Ministry would collate the results of all the budgetary process, and refine the Action and Development Programme accordingly.

Private sector projects are also identified in the Development Programme. The projects selected are all considered financially viable based on the pre-feasibility analyses conducted in the planning study. The Ministry of Tourism would coordinate development of the private sector projects. It would specify the projects and prepare planning and design briefs for them. These briefs would specify the following :

- Nature of the project, and its general or specific location.
- Scale and maximum size of the project, and its space, equipment and facility standards.

- Design and landscaping guidelines.
- Access requirements and utility service standards.
- Programme for development.
- Any other matter of relevance.

When prepared, this list should be submitted to the Uganda Investment Authority. The Ministry would recommend to the Authority that all private sector proposals for implementing the projects in accordance with the briefs should be given favourable consideration for approval. A condition of this approval would be that preliminary sketch designs and plans should be submitted to and approved by the Ministry, before work is allowed to commence. The manual also specifies procedures to be followed for projects proposed in or near national parks. These projects would involve the consideration of the National Park Service. The manual recommends that the Ministry should open discussion with the Uganda Hotels Ltd.—owner and manager of several older hotels—about renovating their properties.

The manual recommends that the Ministry of Tourism should develop a programme for promoting private sector investment in tourism. A high quality investment promotional brochure should be prepared. This brochure would identify all the development opportunities for accommodation projects. The manual specifies the type of information that should be contained in this brochure. The brochure should be made available to investors involved in tourism—both domestic and foreign.

The manual emphasises the importance of plan monitoring and review. These activities would focus on three tasks—continuous monitoring of progress and performance; regularly refining data and adjusting the plan and programme as necessary; and periodically making a formal plan review. The point is made that a critical aspect of plan monitoring is the collection and analysis of sufficient, reliable data. These data would confirm or refute the market projections, tourist characteristics and patterns of behaviour. The planning study contains guidelines for establishing a comprehensive tourism information base.

For monitoring the development programme, quarterly reports on the progress of projects would be made to the Inter-Ministry Coordination Committee. These reports would identify any reasons for project implementation delays, deferments or cancellations. Based on these records, the Ministry would prepare an annual review of the development programme, updating it as necessary and advancing it by a further year. Thus, a 'rolling' five-year programme will be established. Private sector project implementation could be monitored from various sources which are described in the manual.

Biannual reviews of the plan are recommended to be undertaken. Matters to be updated or revised in this review could include the following :

- Projection of tourist arrivals and characteristics over five to 10 years.
- Inventory of tourist accommodation and facilities.
- Programme of tourist accommodation assessed in the light of the revised projections.
- Any revealed necessity to change the emphasis or priorities related to the tourism zones.
- Reassessment of gross and net foreign exchange earning.

The manual recommends that, after a period of about five years, a major plan review should be undertaken. By then, the tourism sector should be sufficiently developed, and accumulated data adequate enough, to provide a sound basis for assessing the progress of tourism and the direction that it is taking. This review should address all the matters dealt with tin the planning study. It should be seen, however, as an updating process and not preparing a new plan. The manual states that the principal purpose of the review would be to test the validity of the application of the plan's principles in detail, not overall. Based on the review, any necessary amendments would be made to the plan, and it would be projected forward for a further five years.

Conclusions

The implementation manual in the Uganda plan represents a more detailed approach to recommending implementation procedures than is usually included in tourism plans. Preparation of a manual such as this is becoming increasingly common. It is very appropriate because of the difficulty experienced by many countries in implementing their tourism plans. The manual is comprehensive—it focuses on procedure which should be followed to implement both the National Structure Plan and the Action and Development Programme, and both public and private sector projects. Other implementation techniques, such as applying development standards and guidelines, are implied in the process set forth in the manual for reviewing development proposals.

The manual justifiably makes a strong point that the National Structure Plan should be adopted by the Cabinet. This gives the plan a legal basis for implementation. Whether the procedure is a two-stage one, as is proposed in the Uganda manual, or one stage—with public review taking place before the initial adoption—depends on the particular circumstances of the country.

The proposed review of the Action and Development Programme is a detailed one, as it should be. This ensures that all concerned parties have the opportunity to be involved in the review, so that the final programme balances all the considerations that need to be made. Identification of the responsible authorities for carrying out specific projects—and the incorporation of these projects into their respective programmes – is an essential aspect of the procedural process, if implementation is to be well coordinated. Specification of the projects by the Ministry of Tourism will encourage that they are included in other agencies' programmes in a proper format.

The approach to development of the private sector projects is a good one, to achieve coordination of these private projects with related public projects. It also gives greater assurance that the private sector projects conform to the plan and programme and meet acceptable development and design standards. To promote private sector investment, the approach recommended of preparing and distributing an investment brochure is a standard one that is commonly applied. The government will need some guidance on where to distribute the brochure internationally, and how to follow up on enquiries.

The manual's recommendations on plan and programme monitoring and review are important. Too often, there is not this type of follow-through on planning. As indicated in the manual, establishing a reliable and comprehensive tourism information system is essential for monitoring. Viewing the development programme as a 'rolling' programme, that is updated every year, is an approach that is increasingly being used. This keeps development programmes viable and current. The proposed biannual and five-year reviews of the basic plan are also very appropriate, in order to maintain a continuously usable plan. Minor adjustments can be made, but the plan's long-term objectives, policies and structures are expected to remain valid. These provide the framework for achieving sustainable tourism development, while still bringing substantial socio-economic benefits to the country.

Conclusions

The case studies represent several different types of countries and regions, and various kinds of tourism situations. The kinds of tourism development—both existing and recommended—also range widely. However, all the case studies reflect an integrated and sustainable development approach to developing tourism. They all reflect tourism being developed based on coherent policy, a logical physical structure plan and progressive institutional elements. The case studies all give great consideration to balancing environmental, socio-cultural and economic objectives. At the same time, they are realistic in recognising the importance of developing tourism that will meet certain market demands. However, they recognise that imaginative new products may also create their own tourist markets, even though specialised ones.

On implementation, the case studies reflect the need to establish firm controls, but within the framework of cooperation between the public and private sectors. Often, divergent development interests must be reconciled. Implementation approaches must often be innovative and tailored to the local circumstances.

Several more specific conclusions can be drawn from the case studies. These can be summarised as follows :

- Carefully planned and managed tourist destinations are much more likely to be successful on a long-term basis than unplanned areas. Planning maintains the viability of tourism resources, with development meeting community and market expectations.
- Tourism planning can be effective for both less and more developed tourist destinations. Planning provides guidelines to less developed countries and regions for

commencing tourism on the right track. It helps already developed places to improve and expand tourism, and often redirects this sector to be more beneficial.

- Effective planning must be based on sound methodological approaches, with application of a sequential planning process. A basic technique in planning sustainable tourism is carrying capacity analysis which, although far from being a perfect analytical tool, provides invaluable guidelines in establishing appropriate types and levels of development for an area.
- Much emphasis is now being given to development of quality tourism. This concept implies protecting the environment, maintaining cultural identity and integrity and achieving a high level of tourist satisfaction, while still generating substantial economic benefits.
- Many possible forms of tourism exist, and they are increasing. A tourism area should consider all these forms of tourism, and select the combination that is most suitable for the environment, society and economy. The most appropriate forms of tourism may also change through time for a particular area.
- Some basic planning principles are applicable in all tourism areas. These principles include establishing tourist gateways, staging areas and tourism zones, clustering attractions and staging development. Adequate transportation facilities are essential to provide proper access to the country or region and convenient travel within the tourism areas.
- Other infrastructure for tourism—water supply, electric power, sewage and solid waste disposal, and telecommunications—must be properly developed in order to provide adequate facilities and services for tourists and prevent environmental problems arising.
- Marketing and product development go hand-in-hand, and must be carefully coordinated to achieve successful tourism development. Tourist markets are becoming increasingly fragmented, and a diversity of imaginative tourism products is being developed.

- Community involvement in tourism is now being recognised as essential. Various successful techniques have evolved to achieve local participation in tourism, and bring direct benefits of tourism to communities.
- Emphasis is now being given to integrating tourism into national, regional and local economies. Techniques for enhancing the economic benefits of tourism, without creating environmental or social problems, are now better understood and being refined.
- Environmental and socio-cultural considerations in tourism can be analysed and programmed in a systematic manner. Much attention is now being given to integrating tourism into the local environment and society.
- Effective approaches for implementation must be emphasised in the planning and development process. Implementation requires not only procedures and techniques, but also political commitment and strong leadership. Adequate financial resources are essential, but many approaches can be applied to secure the necessary funding.
- Carefully coordinated short- and medium-term development programming, that includes both actions to be taken and projects to be developed, is one of the fundamental ways to implement plans.
- Demonstration or pilot projects can be an excellent means of showing how new forms of tourism and development approaches can work. Such projects also provide the opportunities to refine approaches and techniques.
- Organisational structures for tourism must be carefully established, with emphasis on coordination among government agencies and between the public and private sectors. Public-private sector coordination is an essential ingredient in successful implementation.
- Investment incentives—and disincentives—can be a very useful technique to implement development strategies. However, incentives should be applied on a selective basis and modified through time based on changing circumstances.

- All types of education and training are essential for successful tourism, and must be carefully planned and programmed. Persons working in the many aspects of tourism must be properly trained. The general public and people living in tourism areas must be educated about tourism. Tourists must be informed about their destination—its geography, history, cultural patterns and society—and be encouraged to respect it.
- The national and regional governments must often take the initiative in setting development and quality standards for tourism development, in order to ensure that the actual development is implemented properly. However, the local tourism area governments should also be involved in setting and applying appropriate standards.
- Continuous monitoring and management of tourism are essential. Monitoring techniques and procedures should be established early in the development process, and applied to both plan implementation and the on-going progress of tourism. Problems and changing circumstances inevitably arise in tourism development, and monitoring can detect these at an early stage so that appropriate action can be taken. Effective management of tourism is a continuing function and the responsibility of both the public and private sectors.

Tourism planning follows fairly definite procedures and principles, but it is also a continuous process. It involves some experimentation to determine the best specific approaches to be applied in each area. Also, as demonstrated in these case studies, much can be learned from what is being done elsewhere in the world. Although kept reasonably flexible, approaches must still reflect such basic principles as achieving sustainable development, respecting cultural values and spreading economic benefits.

Bibliography

Ashworth, Gregory and Goodall, Brian (eds) (1990), *Marketing Tourism Places*. London: Routledge.

Ashworth, G. J. and Turnbridge, J. (1990), *The Tourist-Historic City*. London: Pinter Publishers.

Boniface, Priscilla and Fowler, Peter J. (1993), *Heritage and Tourism*. London: Routledge.

Bosselman, Fred P. (ed.) (1978), *In the Wake of the Tourist: Managing Special Places in Eight Countries*. Washington, DC.: The Conservation Foundation.

Brendon, P. (1991), *Thomas Cook: 150 Years of Popular Tourism*. London: Seeker & Warburg.

Burkhart, A. and Medlik, S. (1981), *Tourism: Past, Present and Future, 2nd Edition,* Oxford: Butterworth Heinermann.

Burns, P. and Holden, A. (1995), *Tourism, A New Perspective,* Hemel Hempstead: Prentice Hall International.

Cohen, E. (1974), Who is a tourist? A Conceptual Clarification, *Sociological Review* 22(4): 527–555.

Coltman, Michael M. (1989), *Introduction to Travel and Tourism: An International Approach*. New York: Van Nostrand Reinhold.

Coltman Michal M. (1989), *Tourism Marketing*. New York: Van Nostrand Reinhold.

Cooper, Chris, Fletcher, John, Gilbert, David and Wanhill, Stephen (1993), *Tourism: Principles and Practices*. London: Pitman Publishing.

Cooper, C., Fletcher, J., Gilbert, D., Shepherd, R. and Wanhill, S. (1998), *Tourism: Principles and Practice, 2nd Edtion,* Harlow: Longman.

De Kadt, Emanuel (ed) (1979), *Tourism: Passport to Development?* New York: Oxford University Press.

Edgell, David L., Jr. (1990), *International Tourism Policy*. New York: Van Nostrand Reinhold.

Edington, John M. and Edington, M. Ann (1986) *Ecology, Recreation and Tourism.* Cambridge: University of Cambridge Press.

Gee, Chuck Y., Makens, James C. and Choy, Dexter J. L. (1989), *The Travel Industry.* (2nd edn) New York: Van Nostrand Reinhold.

Getz, Donald (1991), *Festivals, Special Events and Tourism.* New York: Van Nostrand Reinhold.

Graburn, N. (1983), The Anthropology of Tourism, *Annals of Tourism Research* 10(1): 9-33.

Gunn, Clare A. (1988), *Tourism Planning.* (2nd edn) New York: Taylor & Francis.

Gunn, Clare A. (1988), *Vacationscape: Design of Tourist Regions.* (2nd edn(New York: Van Nostrand Reinhold.

Gunn, C. (1994), *Tourism Planning: Basics, Concepts, Cases, 3rd Edition,* London: Taylor & Francis.

Hoiloway, J. C. (1998), *The Business of Tourism, 5th Edition.* Harlow: Longman—*Chapters 2 and 3.*

Hudman, Lloyd E. and Hawkins, Donald (1989), *Tourism in Contemporary Society: An Introductory Text.* Englewood Cliffs, New Jersey: Prentice Hall.

Inglis, F. (2000), *The Delicious History of the Holiday.* London: Routledge.

Inskeep, Edward (1991), *Tourism Planning. An Integrated and Sustainable Development Approach.* New York: Van Nostrand Reinhold.

Jafari, J. (1997), Editors page, *Annals of Tourism Research* 5(1): 8.

Leiper, N. (1979), The Framework of Tourism, *Annals of Tourism Research* 6(1): 390–407.

Mill, R. and Morrison, A. (1998), *The Tourism System: An Introductory Text,* Dubuque, Iowa: Kendall/Hunt Publishing.

Pimlott, J. (1947), *The Englishman's Holiday.* London: Faher & Faber.

Smith, V. (ed.) (1989), *Hosts and Guests: The Anthropology of Tourism, 2nd Edition,* Philadelphia: University of Pennsylvania Press.

Towner, J. (1996), *An Hitorical Geography of Recreation and Tourism in the Western World 1540–1940.* Chichester: John Wiley & Sons.

WTO (1998), *Tourism—2020 Vision: Influences, Directional Flows and Key Influences,* Madrid: World Tourism Organisation.

WTO (2000), *Tourism Highlights 2000, 2nd Edition,* Madrid: World Tourism Organisation.

WTO/UNSTAT (1994), *Recommendations on Tourism Statistics,* Madrid: World Tourism Organisation.

